Testimonials

"Transforming an organization takes Leadership, courage, hard work and appropriate methods. This Project has been a success when so many others falter. Understanding how the team achieved this and learning from their implementation is inspirational. It is rare to see such a complete deployment of excellence in action!"

MARK BRACEY
Head of Business Improvement, Lloyds Register Marine

"Having known the methodology for over 10 years, I can say its vision and approach on how to transform a company using process architecture to align the organization are the most advanced I have ever seen. I couldn't be happier to see this vision made reality again through the practical execution of this Project. It answers the question of 'why' with measurable benefits and, more importantly, lays out the map of 'what' and 'how'. I am looking forward to seeing how this continues to drive the performance of Veolia and other companies in the future."

GUNNAR KLEVEN
ABB Power Grids Division, Switzerland Grid Automation, Global Business Unit Head of Quality and Continuous Improvement

"When I saw the Project for the first time, I immediately thought about the big level of effort done on such a broad scale. It's all about people. So, the bottom-up activation through the education of over ¼ of the staff is impressive, and probably the key to success, creating ownership not only for the changes but for the company's results. You have injected a sense of purpose to every employee and that is how sustainable change should be done.

And now, reading the book and understanding what has happened behind the scenes, I see it as a practical guide – trusted to deliver Business Transformation for every manager."

PASCAL STRÖLIN
Head Digital Business Development, UBS Asset Management

"Truly sustainable organizational transformations require an end-to-end vision and approach. This book is an exceptional case study of how to permeate all layers and silos of an organization through data-driven process transformation, and achieve outstanding results, thus proving repeatedly that the investment is worth it. The way process excellence was embedded in the business, and how employees were not only taught but also developed into true champions of the methodology literally make the project worthy of being called a 'textbook example'. It also speaks of the passion and commitment of the team, and how these transformational initiatives require both top-down and bottom-up engagement."

RAUL MORA
Senior Development Excellence Lead, F. Hoffmann-La Roche Ltd

"I witnessed the presentation of the Project several times at several of our North American Operational Excellence Summits. Every time, it was well received by the executive level operations leaders in attendance, and the time for Q & A was never enough. I would like to draw particular attention to the holistic approach of the project – an integrated organizational design combined with the ability to successfully navigate the realities of such a large project. I see the book as a very helpful read for all Business Leaders looking to drive enterprise transformation."

LESLIE ALLEN,
North America IQPC Managing Director

"The structured approach taken by Veolia to fundamentally transform their Business was extremely effective. Really engaging people in the Project, the harmonious link between phases, the use of statistical tools combined with Business Process Architecture are an innovative way to secure the long term sustainability of improvements."

LOPEZ DIAZ-AGUSTIN
SVP Total Customer Satisfaction, Quality, EHS & FES, Faurecia

"Organizational change just got more complex given our era of digitalization and the introduction of Millennials into the workforce. Breaking down change into bite-sized chunks that could be understood by everyone is essential. Veolia's journey has been inspirational in this regard and will serve as a great guide to any other organization embarking on this essential journey of change."

ARAVIND KARTHIGESU
Managing Director ASEAN for ASSA ABLOY

Philippe Roger Louis GUITARD

Jorj-Mădălin MIHAILOVICI

Irina MUNTEANU

Cristian MATEI

Steve TOWERS

DARE!

Behind the Scenes of the Best Business
Transformation Project in the World

Rockstar CX

PUBLISHING

PUBLISHING

Published by Rockstar CX Publishing

United Kingdom

www.rockstarcxpublishing.com

First published in January 2020

ISBN 978–1–9163120–0–5

Quantity sales. Special discounts are available on quantity purchases
        by corporations, associations, and others. For details, contact
        publishing@rockstar.cx

Editor: Ioana Nuțulescu

Illustrations: Andrei Damian (instagram.com/andreiedamian)

Cover design: Faber Studio

Layout design: Faber Studio

Contents

Acknowledgements

We honestly believe that every business is primarily a "people business", whatever its mission might be otherwise.

More than 1 100 people and their hard work made it possible for this Project, its results, the Award it received and ultimately this book to come to fruition. We offer our sincere gratitude to each and every one of them. Unfortunately, we could not name them all here.

However, some stood out; by truly investing their hearts in the project, their involvement went well beyond hard work and contribution:

The people working at Apa Nova, a Veolia company: *Laura Bănică, Olimpia Burghiu, Tatiana Burileanu, Andrei Hoştiuc, Nicolas Lebaron, Mihai Mocanu, Alexandru Moldovan, Iulian Năstase, Dan Pavelescu, Horia Ranetti, Dragoş Stafiescu, Radu State, Adrian Untilă.*

The Advanced Thinking Team: *Bogdan Ardeleanu, Vlad Atanasiu, Elena Dobre, Mariana Drăgilă, Claudiu Florescu, Luiza Ionescu, Cristian C Matei, Renata Moldovan-Borsos, Cristian Nicolae, Cristina Tudor, Mihai Tudor.*

Writing this book has also been a challenge in itself. Piecing the Project together, outlining the methodology, capturing the thoughts and feelings of so many people, and laying all of this on paper in a coherent way was only possible with the support of a great team of people: Advanced Thinking Team, Continuous Improvement Department – Apa Nova and Prior Media Publishing.

Foreword

Why another book about business transformation? The answer is simple: because it is needed. We have seen business transformation projects fail, and being abandoned and forgotten by those who initiated them. In some business communities, these projects are perceived as an "inevitable evil". Therefore, many organizations seem to oppose, avoid or at least try to delay it. In reality, this "inevitable evil" paradigm is just a misconception. Understanding how to use business transformation as a strategic tool is more powerful than any fear of change. And it pays off.

We've all had experience in working for, managing, leading, improving or transforming organizations of all sizes. We have come to understand that in today's fast-paced world, any organizational infrastructure could collapse under the burden of the 21st century challenges. To avoid that, any company should aim for innovation at every level: processes, products, services and business models. We should never assume that what worked for us yesterday will also work tomorrow.

This book is about the exceptional results of a Project based on a clear methodology that led to the reinvention of Veolia's organizational model at local and country level. This is a real-life success story, with the ups and downs of a real down-to-earth business transformation that exceeded all stakeholder expectations. This is also a practical guide that drills down to the how-tos of a proven approach to successfully changing a business model. It is our wish to share it with all of you.

The book tells the story of a sustained 4-year effort that was made possible through the fortunate meeting of its driving forces. We all share the common belief that a business that cannot dream is a business without a future. The plan created for this complete business transformation was executed excellently. The organizational infrastructure was designed to work for the prosperity of a business and not against it. And the seeds to construct such an infrastructure are sown in this book.

People are any company's most prized asset. From the very beginning, hundreds of them were encouraged to contribute to and engage in this ground-breaking approach to business transformation. People were empowered and enabled to express their potential. The trust placed in the local staff paid off as they took on this great responsibility. The transformation of Apa Nova and all other Veolia companies in Romania is a participative process, designed to contribute to the next stage in Veolia's strategic development.

Great achievements are always collective: the more we collaborate, the more progress we make. Everyone involved in the Project proved how collaboration can lead to a better, integrated organizational model that not only meets the requirements of today, but also prepares for the future.

Just like client focus and innovation, the quest for excellence must inform all actions. It is one of the key elements for true business development and growth. This book tells the story of a Project that has been designed from the start with the quest for excellence as an objective – it was envisioned to be globally recognized as one of the best business transformation initiatives, not just within the utilities sector, but across all industries. And it won the title of "Best Business Transformation Project" at the Process Excellence Awards 2019, the most prestigious global competition in its field! At the heart of this transformation lies powerful data, proving its lasting results. It has become a model to be potentially replicated around the world.

The book touches on the essence of an organizational transformation. No matter how promising the acquired knowledge was, it would have been simply unfulfilling to not share it beyond Veolia, so that anyone interested in such an endeavor could learn and benefit from it. Our hope is that the book will provide inspiration and guidance for any manager looking for a trusted model to transform his/her area of work, with local, national, regional or global reach. Knowledge, in this era of shared economy, is the cornerstone of our future growth.

The Project, though, goes beyond the scoping of this first book. It lives, grows and moves in its Continuous Improvement phase, driven by a desire to do better and better. We look forward to seeing this next phase unfold and prove its results, and to witnessing its corresponding book that will outline the blueprint of a self-sharpening organizational model where its strategy can be properly developed and deployed.

The Authors

How to Read this Book

This book is a book of layers. It is born out of an outstanding collaboration between professionals of rather different personalities, expertise and experience, so, naturally, its authors felt it essential to express several things in parallel:

- A primary layer of this book is the real story of a Project which – from being only a dreamer's hope – won the title of **"Best Business Transformation Project"** at the Process Excellence Awards 2019 (Chapters 1, 2, 3), and of a company that, in the span of a few years, changed from being threatened by extinction into a growing regional hub pushing for innovation in the field of business management. It is about leaders who went all in to achieve a 21st century organizational model, a snapshot into the work of more than 2 000 people as they went above and beyond trying to change their fate for more than 4 years.
- On a second layer, this book aims to display the backbone of a proven methodology to redesign any company, in fact any kind of organization – private, government, civil society – in an **integrated** way. It highlights the key concepts that make a significant difference in the way modern management theories can harmoniously be put into practice and even pushed one step further (Chapters 2, 4).
- A third layer introduces a new idea of how to successfully develop, implement and execute Continuous Improvement by capitalizing and sustaining the results of redesigning your business, namely on the process-based Organizational Architecture. By doing so, the vast majority of the problems associated with "standard" Continuous Improvement Programs are dramatically reduced (Chapter 5).
- For a synthetic overview of these key concepts, a fourth layer (**Food for thought**) outlined at the end of each chapter offers a few practical questions to help you understand and apply the concepts presented in this book to your own business reality.
- At the end of the book you will also find a short **Take-away thoughts** section that distils the methodology for those willing to venture into the future. Steve Towers comments on what

works and what doesn't, so as to put the above-mentioned Project in the context of very real management challenges that keep modern leaders up at night.

Beyond all details and layers, we urge you to allow yourself to read this book with an open mind and to join us in a conversation about how to best unlock the true potential that lies in human organization.

Courage to Change

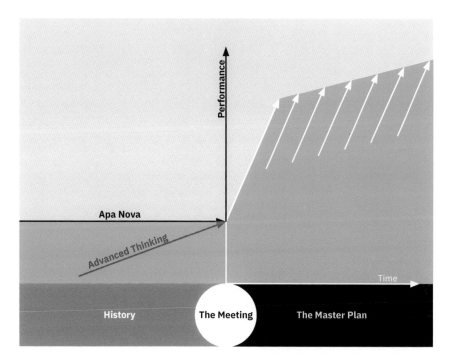

1. Advanced Thinking: Experience and Motivation at the Start of the Project

A fundamental question sparked in 1995, with the search for a PhD subject. At the time, some of the members of the future Advanced Thinking team were studying books and concepts such as Business Process Reengineering, Business Process Management, Total Quality Management, Change Management, Lean Six Sigma and TRIZ, to name only a few. All of these had already stamped their mark on their thinking direction.

Considering the new realities in Central and Eastern Europe at that moment, they began a rather bold inquiry: was it possible that the economies so admiringly seen as "advanced" in the world – and their "advanced" organizations – were in fact not that... advanced?

They were trying to understand why. Apparently, these economies and their organizations provided good products and a good life – at least for some parts of their populations – but something didn't quite match their image before 1989. This is how the idea gained momentum: what if everything – including how the "advanced" economies and their "advanced" organizations were organized and managed – was just an illusion created within an unfortunate specific political and economic context, backed up by the human rights difficulties in Central & Eastern Europe at that time?

This question triggered in 1996 a PhD in Organizational Architecture Reengineering. Even before the Advanced Thinking team was officially formed, some of its future members began to travel the world so as to continuously understand, study, learn and, most importantly, to deeply experience how big and famous organizations work. They saw this venture as a first phase in trying to answer their initial question. This phase came to completion in 2002, resulting in an Organizational Architecture Reengineering Methodology.

Then, step by step, they landed on all continents and began helping lead- ers and their companies – cross-industries, private or state-owned, with or without unions, profit-based or... non-profit based (on paper, of course) – through projects, training, advisory, conferences, coaching, mentoring, seminars, specific support, etc. This second phase ended in 2011 with one of the Advanced Thinking co-founders receiving the special International Quality and Productivity Centre Award for Contribution to the development of the European Improvement Community.

These more than 155 Projects (completed before the Apa Nova Project) included various Country, Regional and Global high level strategic and operational initiatives.

Some of the Projects were the Business Transformation & Turnaround kind of Projects, combining methods and concepts like Strategy Development and Strategy Deployment, Business Process Reengineering, Business Process Management, Organizational (Re)Design, Business Setups, Models and Structures Optimization. Other types of Projects targeted the development and deployment of Operational Excellence Programs – Quality and Continuous Improvement – employing methodologies like KPI Design and Process-Driven Balanced Scorecards, Advanced Root Cause Analysis, 8D, Lean, Kaizen, Six Sigma, Design for Six Sigma and Risk Management.

Both types of Projects were usually supported by specific Change Management Programs and sometimes by the introduction of new technologies and digitalization – large CRM, ERP, SRM implementations, while continuous support and coaching was the norm.

The rest of this section aims to highlight some of the key moments and lessons of the Advanced Thinking Journey of working with over 10 000 managers and employees from the organizations with which they collaborated, as well with their partners and like-minded people from all over the world. These moments and lessons were shared in over 150 conferences, seminaries, lectures and executive boardrooms on all continents and the feedback they received conferred the morality and confidence for them to continue their Journey and the possibility to continuously improve and share their Methodology.

The answer to their initial question took shape when they understood that, fundamentally, the "advanced" economies and their "advanced" organizations suffered from the same fundamental disease like the ones within developing economies, namely the fragmentation of labor and – as a direct consequence – of management. In all of the interactions that the Advanced Thinking team had with these economies and organizations, this fragmentation proved to be at the heart of all performance issues.

Consequently, if not addressing this fragmentation, wave after wave of improvement initiatives will never really solve an organization's fundamental problems, leaving it basically unchanged. Not addressing this fragmentation is the recipe for failure, no matter the name of the improvement initiatives an organization is embarking on. That was a big realization for the Advanced Thinking team, quite crucial.

The answer to this initial question became more profound as they understood that the vast majority of improvement initiatives were themselves developed from the same fragmented perspectives. Therefore, they were approaching organizations in the same fragmented manner; some of them, let's say, from the perspectives of Sales, Finance, HR, some from a Quality or Improvement perspective, some from an Engineering perspective, some regarding digitalization and so on.

In other words, the fragmentation of labor and management also influenced the development of improvement initiatives! For instance, Advanced Thinking believes that slogans like "eating the elephant" or "boiling the ocean" are just a normal consequence of fragmentation in practice as well as in thinking, thus ignoring a holistic approach.

This way of thinking is also linked to the real reach of any function in any organization, which is limited, so that these functions (Sales, Finance, HR, Quality, Improvement, Engineering, Supply Chain, etc.) are pushing vendors to develop and offer solutions for this fragmented perspective. The conclusion is that if there is no synchronization at company level, all these fragmented improvement initiatives will fail sooner or later.

The answer further evolved when the team realized that there is no vendor who sells real integration to a company. They can sell software applications or equipment, they can transfer knowledge, they can advise, they can support, etc., but they cannot sell real integration. So, the only way to achieve it is practically by empowering people to actively participate in the redesigning of their future organization. In turn, this proves to be by far the best way to address resistance to change, which is natural to human beings.

And finally – there is nothing new under the Sun – if the leader of a company and his/her management team fully engage with and commit to change, then the process of transformation is officially set into motion.

A summary of the findings introduced above, in a logical order:

1. These ideas are fundamentals, not only specific to advanced or developed economies, but in the DNA of any organization, no matter the location, existing culture, history, available technology, etc. True, with different intensity, but they are there.
2. These fundamentals can be addressed with an integrated organizational redesign, taking into account all organizational elements in the right order.
3. In turn, this means that if any organization would like to achieve top performance, it can be done.

All of the findings above, crystallized at the end of 2008, finally answered the initial question – yes, the perception of "advanced" economies and their organizations was indeed an illusion. From that moment on, the team got rid of the illusion and preached all over the world that if a company REALLY wants to have exceptional and sustainable results, then it will happen – all potential reasons for it not happening are in fact only excuses.

The process of shaping and building the Advanced Thinking team accelerated in 2004 and was finalized in January, 2014. Over these years, they took on more people with similar beliefs, will power and all the necessary diverse backgrounds and knowledge, from specific leadership and improvement methodologies to psychology and digitalization.

Bearing all of this in mind, they first met the newly appointed management team of Apa Nova on December 22nd, 2015, when Apa Nova was in need of a fundamental transformation of their organization – a static platform that had not been moving for 15 years. However, it had a new leader and a new management team willing to do everything to bring the company back on track, and the majority of employees who waited for the moment to unlock their potential.

The initial agreement between Apa Nova and Advanced Thinking was for the Project to reach the Process Excellence Awards final within the Business Transformation World Summit in the second or third year of their joint effort. The rest is history – together, they won the first place in the world.

2. The Static Platform of Apa Nova

Companies are like ships: we couldn't sail the corporate sea without them. And we need them, because they are vessels of change for the future of business. But sailing isn't always smooth, is it?

Take Apa Nova, for example. Before 2015, Apa Nova – a Veolia company in Romania – was used to sailing calm seas. The captain and executive officers had no strategy, and weren't prepared for rough weather, having the crew perform only daily activities and nothing more.

When the largest wave hit in 2015, the company struggled to keep itself afloat. Its employees were running amok like ducks in a thunderstorm, or like managers fleeing a meeting with their stakeholders. With unclear responsibilities and fragmented processes, it was impossible for the employees to sail the flagship and they risked sinking it into the corporate seabed.

The end-customer saw Apa Nova as a bureaucratic, slow, "old" organization and had a low perception of the quality of its services. At that time, it seemed that the company had no clear vision and was in dire want of a modern strategy of doing business.

Moreover, the captain and the next in command left the crew at the mercy of the elements. There was a desperate need for a new captain, this time a leader, to steer the company out of harm's way. Thus, in 2015, a new CEO was appointed

along with a top management team. They knew it was time for change, and they
armed themselves with the courage to act.

Picture yourself at the helm, in command of a crew of more than 2 000 members who had barely made it through the storm of a lifetime. What would you do to steer the ship back on a course of growth and development, to get it ready for the future?

Would you try to immediately identify the problems and their causes (in other words, patch the holes in the ship and restart its engine)? Or would you go deeper, trying to completely overhaul the ship?

It's obvious that these two options couldn't be more different. If we refer to companies, you need to be fully aware that if you choose to overhaul the ship, you commit to the adventure of completely transforming the company. This is exactly the commitment that the new top management team of Apa Nova was willing to take at the end of 2015. This is how the flagship of all Veolia companies in Romania transformed: the Reengineering Project of Apa Nova.

Now let's take a step back and get a little bit more acquainted with Apa Nova and with its roles in society and on the corporate business stage.

As the world we live in is becoming more aware of how important its resources are and why it is so crucial to preserve them, we all realize that water is far too precious to waste. In fact, water is the essence of life, and this is why companies like Apa Nova play key roles in urban environments all around the world.

As a provider of water services in Bucharest, the capital of Romania, Apa Nova was entrusted with the responsibility of supplying drinking water and with the collection and treatment of wastewater, returning it safely to the environment.

In 2000, the Municipality of Bucharest chose Veolia as a concessionaire of the city's water services for a period of 25 years. It was the result of a public tender, marking the beginning of public-private partnerships in the public utilities sector of Romania. In this way, important international companies with world-class experience in the management of public utilities services could apply and share their know-how more extensively in the benefit of the city of Bucharest.

The Municipality of Bucharest proved to be really visionary at that time, understanding the benefits of such a collaboration between the public and private sectors. Since the beginning, Veolia (represented by Apa Nova) was considered a trustworthy partner, and was constantly granted with the full trust and support of the Municipality.

The company operates under what is considered a landmark concession contract, created with the assistance of the World Bank Group. It was designed as a best practice example of a public-private partnership in 2008, stipulating clear performance targets for all operational and customer-focused processes, which are tightly overseen by the Local Public Authorities.

Apa Nova is part of the Veolia family, the global leader in optimized resource management, with more than 150 years of experience in water services around the globe. Its dedicated professionals work around the clock to resource the city and its more than 2 million inhabitants with clean water.

Today, as part of the community it serves, Apa Nova embraces Veolia's mission of "Resourcing the world" and views itself as a model corporate citizen. It treats water as a heritage and a responsibility, rather than a "product". The consumer is the reason behind all the efforts of the company, thus justifying their motto: "Your water, Our responsibility".

Integrated water services in Bucharest date back to the 19th century. A system for sludge drainage was designed for the first time in Bucharest in 1830, as well as a plan for supplying the city with drinking water, signed by the French engineer Charlier.

50 years later, the Municipal Council decided to bring water from Arcuda (the Bürkli – Ziegler project). An aqueduct was built in order to transport water to the 40 000 m³ reservoir on Cotroceni hill.

In 1887, two major pipelines were installed under two iconic streets in Bucharest, Calea Victoriei Street and Nicolae Bălcescu Boulevard.

Soon after, in 1890, new sources for supplying the city with water were taken into consideration. The civil engineer Elie Radu suggested the use of underground springs, followed by water harvesting and collection works in 1899–1901.

During the First World War, both the distribution network and the equipment were neglected. The works carried out during 1923–1940 (such as collecting water from the Argeș River near Crivina, and using it to supply the city in 1939) ensured an increased reliability of services in terms of pressure and quality.

The Roșu Water Treatment Plant was inaugurated in 1970, and still supplies around 300 000 m³ of water daily. If needed, the capacity can increase up to 520 000 m³ of water.

The construction of the underground wastewater collection Cassette began in the early 1980s; a system of sewage interceptors for collecting and transporting wastewater towards Glina, the location of the Wastewater Treatment Plant.

This was by far one of the most important hydro infrastructure projects ever to be built in a city in Romania.

At that time, Bucharest was going through major transformations: the construction of subway lines was ongoing and major infrastructure plans for preventing the frequent overflows of the Dâmbovița River were also underway. The solution was to alter the path of the river by building a concrete riverbed, housing major concrete sewage interceptors beneath it.

In 2011, 11 years after Apa Nova became the concessionaire of the water supply and sewage services of the Bucharest Municipality, the company was entrusted with the concession of the Glina Wastewater Treatment Plant and the main sewage interceptors, built under the Dâmbovița River, winding across the entire city. This was a great responsibility for the company, given all of the environmental requirements. Moreover, the grand project of building those sewage interceptors – which started in the early 1980s – had never been finished.

In order to make this project fully operational, considerable investments had to be budgeted for the next few years. This meant finalizing the fitting out works for the discharge of sewage interceptors into the Dâmbovița River and the Glina Treatment Plant, unclogging the interceptors and eliminating the major bottlenecks, and implementing a uniform development strategy by effectively managing the wastewater collection and transport system (Radu, I., Șendroiu, C., 2013).

In 2012, complex works were executed on the wastewater Cassette, including the removal of 23 out of the 25 major bottlenecks identified along its path and connecting the sewage interceptors with the Dâmbovița River (Radu, I., Șendroiu, C., 2013). At that time, this endeavor was considered the most important hydro-infrastructure project in Romania, and probably in the entire CEE region.

Since its early days, Apa Nova managed to keep up with the city's continuous development, providing services to new clients. Although achieving all the operational targets stipulated in the concession contract, something was not going so well.

The only vision provided by previous management teams was to manage things in such a way as to meet the requirements of the concession contract. To them, what happened after their mandate was of no consequence. Hence, a holistic business transformation Project was utterly utopian.

To the regional leaders, this way of doing business was a static platform that lasted 15 years in a row. The company didn't keep up with all the requests and objectives that came from the Regional Headquarters. Previous management teams tried to show the regional managers only positive aspects. They tried to hide all the problems they faced while managing the company.

Furthermore, the Organizational Structure of Apa Nova was nothing but a collection of unrelated boxes in an organizational chart. This led to management having a fragmented view of the entire company. Because of that, several improvement initiatives, fragmented by default, had been implemented over the years, with no significant results. In fact, this only meant patching up the ship, not overhauling it.

The big shift happened at the end of October, 2015. The top management team had just been replaced, which had brought the company on the edge of collapse. In a board room full of anxious managers, the situation was very tense: it was critical to put the right people in charge of restarting Apa Nova.

The newly appointed CEO welcomed this challenge and made it his mission. "Courage to change" was written on his mandate. He made a promise to start a Reengineering effort with a clear vision and strategy, to ensure a great future for the company. This was not only unprecedented at Apa Nova, but also unthinkable until that moment. Once again, the Municipality of Bucharest proved to be a real partner, encouraging the company to embark on this Journey.

To make this happen, the first step he took was to appoint a new local management team. The second step was to obtain the necessary support from middle management and informal leaders to embrace the Reengineering effort. Those who wouldn't get involved in the Transformation Project were asked to leave the organization.

This was the full story of Apa Nova until 2015, the moment when this Project started. To transform a static platform into a 21st century organization model is not an easy task. It needs time and energy from all parties involved. It needs a strong management team with courage and vision. It also requires responsible employees with the right mindset to change their work and their views on how things are and how they should be done. But none of the above would work without a well-designed plan.

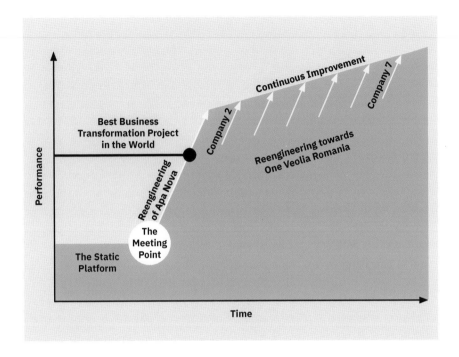

As mentioned earlier, at the end of 2015, the Advanced Thinking team received a phone call from the HR department of Apa Nova. They requested a meeting to discuss a Lean Six Sigma training course for their management team. Right from the start, there was a creeping feeling that this was not going to be a typical discussion between an HR department and a consulting firm. On behalf of Apa Nova, the newly instated top management team attended the meeting, having a difficult mission – their mandate was to get the company back on track. In other words, to be on a track of business growth and development.

All elements fell into place for Apa Nova and Advanced Thinking to join forces towards such an ambitious goal.

What Did "Bringing the Company Back on Track" Require?
After a short meeting, every single member of the top management team agreed that what they wanted first and foremost was to work on themselves; they wanted to learn everything with utmost efficiency so they could achieve a meaningful and valuable business transformation. It became obvious that in

order to fulfill that ambition, a more holistic and inclusive approach was necessary. Not only those in charge, but the entire company had to learn, feel and contribute to the transformation.

Before crafting the actual plan, it was essential to have a realistic image of the genuine situation of the company. Consequently, an organizational assessment was deployed for Apa Nova, evaluating the maturity of the organization from several perspectives: Strategy & Leadership, Organizational Design, Product and Service Design, Risk Management, Performance Management, Quality & Continuous Improvement, Learning & People Development. Having a clear picture of the state of affairs in the company at that time was the perfect prerequisite to begin planning the Project.

It was critical to create a workable plan, with the right approach, which would take everything into consideration. Planning for success would become a reality. While evaluating the state of affairs at that time in the company, the common decision was to redesign the identified processes by applying a common-sense approach. A "first pass" simplification of the existing processes only implied basic knowledge transfer to simplify and to eliminate redundancies, unlike a rigorous Lean Six Sigma redesign approach at that moment in time.

Planning was essential for this endeavor and the transformation began with the creation of a 5-year Master Plan meant to not only bring one company back on track, but to also design a best-in-class country business setup. Based on the results of its implementation, this business setup would be able to compete with any top performing organization in the world.

Several key principles guided the careful construction of the Master Plan: first and foremost, when starting the complete redesign of a company, you need to really understand its external conditions: who are the stakeholders, what and how much do they ask of the company? Only by answering these driving questions could the company be redesigned in an integrated way in order to meet the expectations of its stakeholders.

Another imperative ingredient when embarking on such a journey is the right mindset. Everything was planned in a way that would involve as many employees as possible from the very beginning of the Reengineering Project. This led to a massive shift in thinking, which ultimately caused a shift in practice.

Last, but not least, the design of each organizational element, in the right order, aimed to improve and sharpen the preceding elements. People were directly involved in designing the Organizational Architecture. The more their mindset changed, the faster their learning curve progressed and they became more accepting of the change ahead. With their new understanding, the quality of their work was always continuously improving. This domino effect enabled the continuous sharpening of previous work.

The Master Plan was the blueprint of how the integrated design was to unfold and it was based on three pillars:

1. **Day by Day Management Excellence** – creating a new Organizational Architecture for Apa Nova and afterwards for all Veolia companies in Romania, which meant building a new foundation for the future organization, element by element;
2. **Operational Excellence** – creating a Continuous Improvement engine to sustain the new organization, aiming for a self-sharpening mindset, empowering people to always look for ways to improve their work;
3. **Strategic Excellence** – completely redesigning the Strategy Development and Strategy Deployment processes to enable, align and support the Strategy Execution, based on the Process-Driven Organizational Architecture.

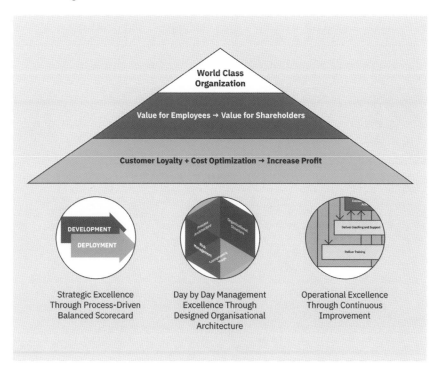

The Master Plan

The order in which these three pillars are approached is directly influenced by the findings of the maturity assessment of the organization. The organizational context sets the frame for a correct approach: the foundations of the organization would be redesigned first, leading to Day by Day Management Excellence.

Continuous Improvement would be set up and trained as a muscle to create a culture of continuous, disciplined change, leading to Operational Excellence. According to this new mindset, structured Strategy Development and Strategy Deployment processes would be put into place to guide the organization into the next cycles of development, leading to Strategic Excellence.

Day by Day Management Excellence:
Creating a New Organizational Architecture

Ask 100 managers how their organization came to be. The vast majority will answer that organizations today, most of the time, just happened as a result of wave after wave of ad-hoc restructuring, reorganizing, down-sizing, etc. No one actually designed them to perform at their best. The ones that grow into large corporations, grow in a similar manner, adding bits and pieces in order to face the constant challenges of a dynamic, high-speed environment, without an overall perspective on integrating the new elements.

Just like this patched airplane above, these organizations work, but all the patching and fragmentation generate enormous costs, often unseen and unperceived. Statistics show that more than 75% of the activities happening within an organization are non value-added activities. Seventy five percent!

Considering this, the very first step in creating a highly functioning organization is to completely reengineer its Organizational Architecture so it can support all future developments and deliver outstanding results. Mainly, an Organizational Architecture consists of the following elements: Processes Architecture, Process-Driven Organizational Structure, Process-Driven Balanced Scorecard and KPI Architecture, Risk Management, Job Descriptions, and an Integrated Management System. All of these elements are taken into account, and redesigned in a fully integrated way, working with everyone involved, at every level in the company.

Once the setup for one company proved to be effective, the plan was to expand the conversation country-wide, and to create an integrated business setup for all the Veolia companies in Romania.

The complete redesign of one company is an act of courage for any top management team. Even if the end result is more effectiveness and efficiency in the company – apparently a win-win scenario for all parties involved – those who drive such an initiative consciously enter a war against the status-quo, against comfort, against "works just fine". Multiply this by the number of Veolia companies in Romania and imagine the amount of courage and stoicism this newly appointed top management team had when deciding to enter this path.

Operational Excellence: Creating a Continuous Improvement Engine

It's a fact that if you observe any well-performing system that benefits from no actions of nurturing, sustaining and improvement, you will see that the system will degrade over time. Moreover, after any transformation is completed, usually all parties involved need time to absorb, process and adopt the changes; employees and customers alike. To create a sustainable transformation, a period of active rest and consolidation of results needs to be planned and put into practice.

Following the design of the Organizational Architecture, it is necessary to adopt a structured approach to enable a Continuous Improvement mindset for the organization and all its elements. To make Continuous Improvement an effective pillar for an organization, it is essential to clearly envision and execute the Continuous Improvement process. Some critical aspects must be tackled:

- Selecting the improvement initiatives that contribute to a clear set of organizational KPIs, perfectly aligned to the overall strategy and objectives;
- Developing the internal capability to manage and lead those initiatives, by training a cross-functional group of employees;
- Creating one single project portfolio management for those actions, thus avoiding fragmentation and overlaps in improvement initiatives;
- Objectively showing the actual business benefits of every improvement action.

Strategic Excellence: Completely Redesigning the Strategy Development and Deployment Processes

By building on the Organizational Architecture and Continuous Improvement, Apa Nova would design and deploy its strategy in such a way as to move the company from a predominantly Management-by-Control attitude to Collaborative Leadership, directly derived from the company's processes. Strategy Development, Strategy Deployment and Strategy Execution exist in order to effectively manage organizations in their entirety; they are supposed to guide decision-making, enable transparent actions and create a Process-Driven Balanced Scorecard that integrates priorities.

When a Stakeholder-Driven Organizational Architecture is put into place, the Balanced Scorecard derives directly from the stakeholders' needs. When deploying a Process-Driven Balanced Scorecard, the concept of stakeholders stands at its DNA. Having a KPI Architecture that fits both the Process Architecture and the Organizational Structure like a glove creates a framework which ensures that the company is on the right track to meeting the set objectives. Having both horizontally and vertically aligned KPIs shatters any possible conflicting interests, such as organizational goals that directly contradict individual performance requirements.

With this mindset and these tools for Continuous Improvement at the core of the organization, managers are empowered to timely report any deviations from the goal and to immediately implement corrective actions.

Once all elements fit into place and are supported by a process-driven budgeting system, it becomes much more likely to achieve correctly cascading objectives, proper monitoring, timely adjustments and the involvement of every organizational level.

Strategy Development, Strategy Deployment and Strategy Execution are used for communicating and achieving goals, throughout the company. For this to work, a clear strategic vision is necessary because planning is thought out for the long-term. Then, working teams develop and detail shorter term objectives to pave the way to the long-term goal.

The foundational elements of a world-class organization and the way the methodology approaches the complete reengineering of any company enable an efficient use of Strategy Development, Strategy Deployment and Strategy Execution. In this way, anyone, at any level of the organization, will be able to thoroughly understand his/her role and contribution to the final result. This creates the opportunity for everyone to actively participate in goal setting.

People at the Core of the Business Transformation Effort

The large majority of transformation initiatives end up in failure[1]. Failure to deliver, failure to adapt, failure to sustain. It is generally accepted in the field of Business Transformation that projects fail because people don't usually respond well to change. Novelty and the unknown can induce this kind of resistance. As Margaret Weathy and Myron Kellner-Rogers point out: "the resistance we experience from others is not to change itself. It is to the particular process of change that believes in imposition rather than creation."

People are the makers and breakers of any good strategy, because every business is, in the end, a people business. While the methodology for setting the technical elements of the organization in place is a crystal clear, structured approach (as detailed in the following chapters), what makes any transformation project of this magnitude are the people actually working throughout the change. Being able to engage people in a meaningful way is essential for ensuring the success of such an initiative. By involving people from the very start, enabling collaborative creativity and individual contribution, recognizing differences and celebrating breakthroughs, the Project would be set up for success.

It ultimately boils down to two driving vectors that enable successful change within an organization: the capacity to embrace change and the ability to sustain it. For a project to succeed, both have to be addressed.

Just visualize the wheels of a car in motion, always adapting to the texture and curves of the road. This adaptation requires continuous coordination and the ability to maintain balance. In the case of Apa Nova, the balance must be

1   73% of Business Transformations fail (according to a McKinsey & Company study published in 2015), down from 80% in 2012.

struck between business continuity (the existent state) and business transformation (the desired future state). The true redesign of a company can occur only by unlocking its organizational potential and by encouraging people to work together, and at their best. It turns out, people cannot begin such a complex undertaking without someone setting the tone for change.

Setting the tone for change is the main role of leadership at the start of a project. And to satisfy this role you need to communicate the right messages, at the right moment in time. Some call this a vision, some call it a mission, a call to action, a change blueprint, a transformation charter and many other things. Whatever the name, in order to get people on board, a few elements need to be very clearly articulated and incessantly communicated:

- Why the organization cannot keep doing things the same way as it has been and what the consequences could be – this should create a sense of urgency and get people moving from where they are;
- What the organization needs to reach – this should create a sense of pull towards the future, a standard against which to measure the efforts for change. The goal should be measurable and bold;
- The Master Plan – the right-sized roadmap, not too lenient, not too strict, which creates enough certainty to set the pace for progress and is flexible enough to allow for substantial change and innovation in the DNA of the organization.

At the beginning of the Project, as part of the organizational assessment, potential threats were identified by conducting a survey to capture the voice of the company's employees and their concerns. The results of this survey showed that a high number of employees reported unclear roles and responsibilities, inconsistent Job Descriptions, and unbalanced workload and remuneration policies.

At the same time, the survey sought to reduce the waste of skills. The honest discussions about such issues were enough to create a sense of urgency, yet too small to build a coalition. In order to prevent any pitfalls, the top management team of the company allowed their employees to co-create the necessary new reality and to develop complete and sustained communication throughout the Project.

Even if many people were motivated to surmount the hurdles, many found themselves otherwise confused, asking *"but what actually needs to change?"*

The answer lies in this book and consists of "all of the elements of the organization". But that is a hard pill to swallow all at once, isn't it?

Step by step, people had to understand each element, how each element links to the next, and then how it all fits together. Starting from the creation of the Master Plan, the people of Apa Nova were immersed in a process of continuous Learning and Development. It began with the transfer of "technical" knowledge, which was later backed up by Project support & coaching during meetings. The entire learning process was designed to develop competencies to better face and sustain the change happening in the organization. Later in the Project, Learning and Development focused even more on the development of specific soft and transversal skills.

It was like a constant fulcrum, providing know-how individually or in teams, through open-hearted group dialogue or face to face interactions, or by any technological means that a co-worker in the Project might have needed. The Project would be run by the people and with the people, making the change theirs.

Food for thought:

- Is the need for change present and real in your organization, enough to embark on such a journey?
- Do you personally dare to embark on such a journey and do you have the grit to see it through?
- What would the necessary ingredients be in order to ensure a successful transformation?
- Who are the key-players that enable a business transformation?
- How would you go about transforming your own business, while taking into account all realities and constraints?

Change in Action: Building the 21ˢᵗ Century Organization

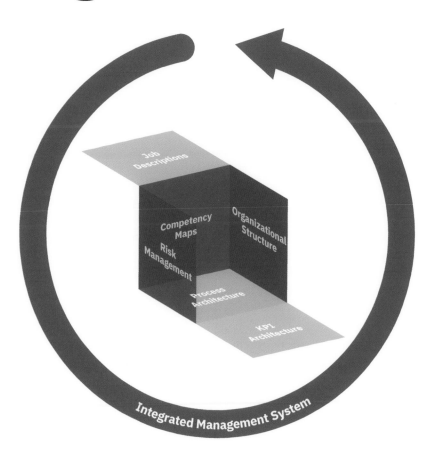

Imagine you're at work on an icy Wednesday morning and you're invited to a workshop called "Operational Reengineering of the Company." You sit down next to your co-workers. Some of them, you know; others you've never met. They are certainly diverse. They introduce themselves, and it's obvious they're coming from all areas of the organization, from different levels. Some seem highly experienced, while others have recently joined the company.

Ten minutes into the kick-off meeting, you're invited to rethink all the aspects of the company you work for. Everything. You, and everyone else in the room. How would you feel? That's what happened for the employees of Apa Nova on the 13th of January, 2016. The reactions across that room were as chaotic as you may think, ranging from long faces to big smiles. A deluge of questions began flowing as if torrential rain just hit the desert:

> *"But why would we change? Everything is going well!"*
> *"What will change for me and the people I work with?"*
> *"What are the precise steps of this Project? When will it end?"*
> *"It's been done before and it never really worked, why would it work this time around?"*
> *"Can I tell my co-workers about this?"*
> *"Who is going to work on this? How are we supposed to fit it into our work schedule, when we're already so busy?"*
> *"Why do we need to think about that?"*
> *"Why is the plan set up like this?"*

Behind each question, there was something more than just the need to know what was going on. It was a deafening chorus of concern and enthusiasm, of disbelief and blind faith, of retraction and encouragement.

These questions were natural, and the top management team had already prepared some critical messages before the kick-off meeting. These messages, as well as the technical answers to each key question that came up were concertedly repeated throughout the day, with a top-notch mix of honesty, openness and determination. This was essential to convince people to go along with the plan. The kick-off meeting for the Reengineering Project lasted for two full days and involved more than 95 people.

Are We Really Doing This?
One curious thing happened: somehow, many believed that the Project was a secret that only those invited to the meeting should know about, in spite of

the fact that everyone who participated was encouraged to go back into the organization and spread the word. A few weeks into the Reengineering Project, it became obvious that many areas of the company still didn't know anything about it.

The top management team organized a one-day event with almost 200 participants. The plan for the Project was laid out again and even more questions and concerns sprang out of the crowd, all addressed and answered afresh. The room only went silent for a moment, after several intense hours of discussion. Suddenly, a voice hit the nail on the head: *"are we really doing this?"* The members of the top management team shared one decisive glance among each other, and within a quarter of a second, answered in unison: *"YES!"*

As the story developed, so did the craving for actual results. The people investing time, brain cells and emotions into the Project were dying to see their work materialize. The top management team was set on changing a static company into a company designed to thrive in the global economic landscape of the 21st century.

They made it clear from the start that everyone's fears and concerns would be immediately heard and addressed, and they repeated it on every occasion. At one point, during a long and tiring review with more than 40 managers, a member of the top management team addressed the elephant in the room: *"Maybe some of you hoped that this was just an exercise, a simulation. But we're actually doing this! All the things you design today will become our reality tomorrow. Treat this Project with the utmost seriousness, it will impact us all."* Any bit of doubt had to be eliminated.

Moving on to the technical aspects, this chapter introduces all the organizational elements that must be addressed in the **integrated design** of any company, institution, NGO or any other human endeavor. In practice, they should all be approached together, level by level, and taking into consideration the way they interact. But this implies **understanding** all of them and how they work together, which is quite difficult without further information. So, they will be presented one at a time, with examples from the Apa Nova experience of design and implementation.

A complete redesign of all organizational elements, in their entirety, could prompt any manager to think that he/she is dealing with another attempt at "boiling the ocean". Yet, when done right and following a structured approach, an integrated Organizational Architecture becomes an achievable outcome. This book shows a path towards the integration of all organizational elements and resolves the prevalent mislabeling of such an initiative as "boiling the ocean".

To help you better navigate this chapter, the map below presents an integrated way of looking at organizational elements and how they are all interconnected.

1. Who Cares? Stakeholder Identification

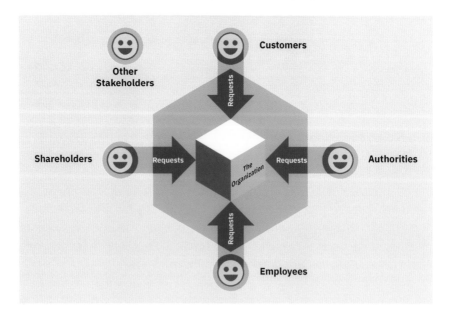

What makes a successful organization? If you ask different people, you will get different answers pointing out different organizational elements, based on past experiences when their organization was "doing well". Some will say: *we were the most successful when the entire organization focused on performance metrics and how to best measure and report them.*" Others will say: *"we were the best management team when we were leading the market."* Others will talk about vision, strategy, operational excellence, etc.

But if you take a step back and really think about it, these answers don't get to the essence of the question. It's like asking *"what makes my soup the best?"* and someone saying *"it has the perfect amount of salt in it"*, instead of *"it reminds me of my childhood."* The first answer addresses the HOW of soup-making instead of the WHY of soup-making. In this way, we might get lost in solutions and fail to set the appropriate benchmark for a successful organization. So, what makes a successful organization?

We believe the answer is surprisingly simple: when it satisfies all stakeholder needs. This was the first high-level conversation in the Project, to help the top management team of Apa Nova understand how to think about everything that was going to change. With that in mind, their actions throughout the Project would strengthen Apa Nova as a Stakeholder-Driven Organization.

First of all, the Operational part of the Reengineering Project was set up around the most important types of stakeholders. One member of the top management team took on the responsibility of making sure all processes that would address one particular stakeholder would be taken care of. The main types of stakeholders were: Customers, Shareholders, and Authorities. The team also agreed that they would work together to address internal stakeholders, such as Employees.

One thing that the top management team did – which made a world of difference – was to "represent" the stakeholder's voice throughout the Project. For example, one member of the top management team attended every Project review meeting and, as people were greeting him, he would always say: *"Please don't bother to get up, I'm only a customer of Apa Nova. I'll just sit here listening, maybe I'll ask some questions if that's okay."* During the meetings, he used this idea again and again, in almost every intervention.

It had a tremendously positive effect, constantly reminding everyone: *"who are we doing this for?"* Personifying the stakeholder made it relatable. It also gave the stakeholder the proper authority in the room because the person who was taking on this role was a truly respected authority figure within the company.

The customers of Apa Nova thought the company was underperforming. Knowing this, the top management team decided to do something revolutionary in the utilities sector in Romania: they organized a public consultation named *Let it be clear*, and they invited their customers to express their needs and grievances. They booked the largest indoor hall in Bucharest (over 4 000 seats) and sent out invitations to the representatives of their stakeholders. They also made sure that a few hundred employees were there, all the managers from all levels of the company, plus everybody active in the Reengineering Project.

Having invited the public media, they actually met their customers – the entire room was full of people: individual customers, owner association representatives, large private developers, representatives of hospitals, schools, large public institutions, and even other utilities providers. And all of them had something to say – the meeting lasted almost an entire day, with dozens of issues raised and discussed. It was set up as a reality check from the outside-in, and from the inside-out. This kind of consultation meetings became common practice, the new way in which Apa Nova was building the relationship with its customers.

Similar consultation meetings were undertaken with all other stakeholder groups: Public Authorities, Shareholders (including the Municipality of the City of Bucharest), Employees and their representative organizations. Each had their say, either renewing previous engagements, or expressing new expectations.

The Reengineering of Apa Nova was about to happen under the freshly reinforced pressure from all its stakeholders. As it should have been. It was time to prove that the company was able to address and work with all of them.

All the information thus collected was distilled and translated into specific requirements, and gradually shared in the beginning of or within the process that addressed it. The success of the Reengineering Project would be based on the satisfaction of all these needs. In the end, all the processes had to be designed to satisfy all stakeholder needs.

A Customer-Driven Organization is obviously built having the customer in mind. Nevertheless, reality means more than the customer. So many other stakeholders with so many other needs and requests come into play on a strategic level. The conversation about organizational transformation should start with properly understanding the market environment. Who are your stakeholders and what do they want from you?

Understanding what they want in business terms means being able to translate their voice into measurable outcomes. At the start of the Project, Apa Nova was under immense pressure from all stakeholders.

2. What It Is that We Do: Creating the Process Architecture

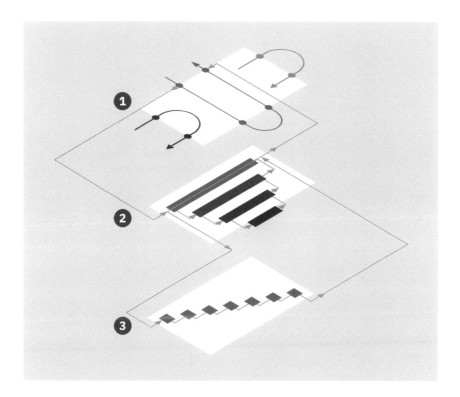

A. From Functional Thinking to Process Thinking:
Why Do We Need to See Our Processes?

Process, Work, Value Stream, Flows are all words we use for "what it is that we do here". Looking from the outside-in, from the perspective of customers and other external stakeholders, what the organization does is what the organization is. In other words, what an organization does is its very essence. In order to make a meaningful, profound change in an organization, we should start by changing what we do and how we do it. But what does the company actually do? And what should it be doing?

First and foremost, making the right decisions! It's January, 2016. A new management team comprised of experienced managers is set to revolutionize a traditional company gone awry. With a tight deadline and one shot at hand, they took up the challenge of allowing their core management beliefs to crumble, and opened up to a transformation and a journey to unlearn and relearn what it meant to really Reengineer their company. Not everyone knew that their Management Contract was directly connected to bringing the company back on track.

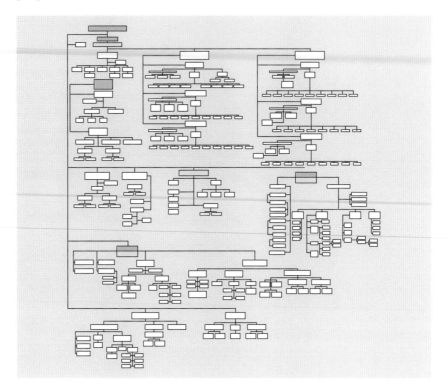

The Organizational Chart of Apa Nova at the start of the Project

The top management team was faced with a simple group exercise: a new customer wants a water services contract with Apa Nova. Using the current organizational chart, they were asked to map the path for this request as it was attended to within the company, at that time:

- Who is responsible with receiving the request and beginning the process of fulfilling it?
- Who then is the second one, the third, the fourth, etc.?
- Which role is the last on this chain of transforming a request into an output: fulfilling the customer's need?

The organizational chart was printed on multiple A0 sheets and taped together into a 50 square foot poster. One member of the top management team drew in red the flow of transforming a request into a new contract, on the organizational chart: the result was a maze. From the first contact point to the end, the process developed through nine different structures with no apparent logic other than the historical ad-hoc setting of the company. A maze that was not following, by any means, any principles of efficiency for an organization functioning in the 21st century.

The next obvious question when faced with such a maze was: *"Who is responsible for delivering to the customer, from the very first moment a request reaches the company until the very last moment before it reaches the customer?"* The members of the top management team took a long look at each other and answered with a sigh: *"NOBODY in particular."* This meant that the process was, so to speak, like an orphan: there was no one to look after it. And it became obvious that someone should be.

This was a fragmented organization. The newly appointed CEO said: *"I have been trying to understand the current Organizational Structure for over a year. The only conclusion I reach every time is that it's a collection of fiefdoms, everyone in charge of unrelated fragments within the company, in spite of our common goals."* One member of the top management team stood up, walked across the room to the huge poster and ripped it off the wall and into half. Someone else remarked: *"I would draw an organizational chart on a piece of paper in 10 minutes, without a second thought. It never occurred to me there should be principles behind designing the Organizational Structure!"*

In that moment, everyone understood. A siloed thinking, with all its inherent problems, wasn't going to work for Apa Nova. They were now set on challenging every aspect of the "old", so as to rebuild the company from its core. It was time for a change! It was time to redesign the company. It was time to move away from functional thinking and on to process thinking.

In other words, the stakes were clear. Everyone desired a complete turnaround on a strategic level, but for that to be achieved, the company had to be organized in such a way as to best fulfil all stakeholder needs.

For that to happen, you need more than a top management team. You need to mine into the collective knowledge of the people who work together in the trenches of the organization, the ones executing the processes that deliver actual results. For a real transformation to occur, top-down decisions have to be paired with concrete and practical bottom-up knowledge of how the organization actually works towards meeting stakeholder needs.

B. Process Identification: The Top-Down Approach

There were over 25 top and middle managers from all departments of Apa Nova, sitting around the table. It was one of the early review meetings of the Project and there was quite a large amount of information that had been presented up to that point. Seemingly tired and frustrated about not seeing the end of the meeting, one member of the top management team stood up, waited for the room to be quiet and asked: *"What is it that we do around here?"*

People sighed, thinking that he had not been listening through the hours of presentations that had gone by. Still, he looked around the room trying to meet everyone's gaze and insisted on an answer. People started to present everything again, pointing at the process maps on the walls. Some even read the details of the process maps out loud again.

He was not satisfied. He wanted another answer. A simpler answer. Not simplistic like *"we provide water to the citizens of Bucharest"*, which he knew was an over-simplification for an organization of 2 000+ employees. He wanted something less detailed than what each employee does, but more thorough than the name of one service provided by the company. Still, it was the question itself that was important.

What he was trying to do was to get people moving from the role-level and department-level process mapping to the company level, even if they weren't going to think of the right answer on the spot. He knew this, because the top management team had done that specific high-level exercise under the guidance of Advanced Thinking.

They had been asked to identify all the processes of the company, starting with each stakeholder request and ending with the satisfaction of that request. After getting through about 30 processes, they realized there was much more to add. Some requirements were placed by different stakeholders on the same process and there were bits of processes they could not fully grasp from the beginning to the end, because some of the work was "hidden" within the lower levels of the organization.

Furthermore, they realized the true meaning of the exercise – knowing the full list of processes in the company is the only way to know what had to be managed and improved in order to bring the company back on track. According to the high-level principle that they adopted for Change Management within the Project, they would have to create this list, working with the people at Apa Nova.

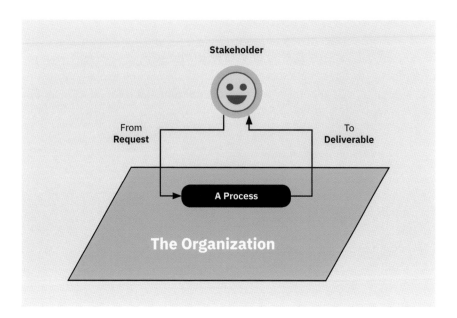

Process Identification

Identifying a company's processes is everyone's job – it implies listing all the responsibilities that an organization has to its stakeholders and to itself, everything that needs to be managed so that the company operates successfully. The exercise that the top management team of Apa Nova had to do was one of top-down Process Identification. It meant starting with all the known requirements that all stakeholders place on the company, and naming the processes that address them.

This is remarkably useful when designing a company from scratch. But that wasn't the case for Apa Nova. Its real processes were scattered and tangled together in the current Organizational Structure and in people's minds. For the Reengineering Project to succeed, they needed to be discovered as they were and then untangled by the people managing and executing them day by day. This way, there would not only be clarity about what the company needs to do, but there would also be a shared understanding between all levels of management within the organization.

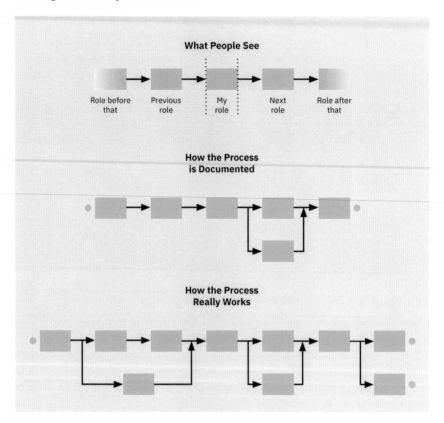 46

C. Process Discovery: The Bottom-Up Approach

It is a well-known fact that the knowledge of an organization lives in the minds of its employees. Most organizations today are "heavily documented". Multiple procedures, work instructions and guidelines exist, as well as many strategies and workflows that are meant to guide and instruct, but most of the time they are forgotten, rarely used or useful.

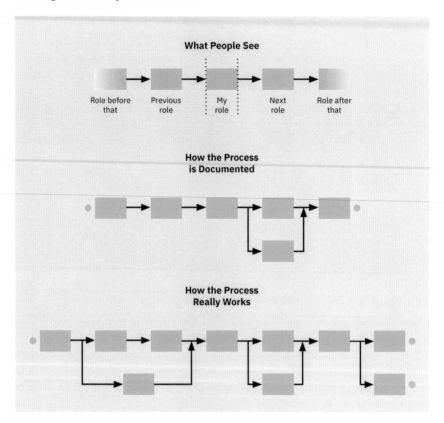

Different perspectives on the same processes

The truth about how an organization truly operates lies within the expertise of its employees. That is often a source of power for the individual working in an organization, a leverage in securing his/her job – no one could ever reproduce exactly the work that one individual does, in order for the process to reach its designated results. It was time to empower people. And what better way to see how the real work is done than encouraging employees to map their **real** processes?

Process mapping is not a new method in the world of management; it's been around since the 1920s. Still, process mapping is most often an incomplete exercise. You can never really see everything you would like to see. As Alfred Korzybski famously remarked, *"the map is not the territory"* and arguably, there is no reason why it should be. Elaborate process maps are difficult to build. Also, in a real-life Reengineering Project, one has to keep in mind that the processes will change considerably shortly after the initial mapping is finished – so many details of the current situation might simply become irrelevant as soon as the processes change. The key is to map the processes with **just enough** details, taking into account all the existing realities. Moreover, mapping is the beginning of a long journey meant to address all the elements of the organization, thus, more details can be added along the way.

Mapping the actual work has to become a basis for the future, integrated with other organizational elements like KPIs or Job Descriptions, which will be described in detail in the following sections. So, what are the next elements that are critical to transforming an organization in an integrated way?

Process Roles: Responsibility at the Lowest Level
By the time a team is built, everybody expects that its members **will know exactly what their roles are, so that the team will work well together.** But this is often easier said than done in the business field. The top management team of Apa Nova wanted this on a grand scale – they requested that each employee in the organization should know all of his/her roles. More than 2 000 employees! Furthermore, they needed to know if they had the right number of people for what they intended to do. A daunting proposal with a pivotal solution: Process Roles.

Advanced Thinking proposed a customized Process Mapping Standard that went beyond the classical swim-lane/departmental division of authority, right down to the lowest level of responsibility in the company – the individual process role. Applied to all the processes of the company, this solution opens up a world of possibilities in terms of implementation, performance management, Learning and Development, even in making the future Organizational Structure more viable and flexible, as will be described in the following sections of the book.

But for now, it's important to understand how this solution was made possible. A simple, workable definition of process role had to be shared amongst the hundreds of people who would be mapping the processes. What people seemed to understand best was that a process role implies that one type of person does one type of work. It represents the lowest level of responsibility in a process, and it includes all the activities for which one type of employee is responsible, from the point the process role is triggered by a request until it has completed its work, and the responsibility goes on to the next person. At this point, a new process role is triggered, continuing the process. This definition is designed to help practitioners avoid pitfalls that may hinder their actual work in the field, such as:

1. People misunderstanding that each small activity may be done in an individual style, as a process role in its own right. This misconception could lead to artificially mapping too many process roles, thus expressing the same thing with different words;

2. People misunderstanding process roles as the sum of their responsibilities or of the activities that they do; in the case of Apa Nova, the second pitfall tended to trap more people. Early process maps had process role names like "engineer", "plumber" or "manager", which are in fact positions in the Organizational Structure;

3. People misunderstanding the correct scope of one process role, so that they mapped two or more process roles into one (with implications such as unclear responsibility, incorrect KPIs, hidden deliverables, incorrect Job Descriptions, and so on), or creating a process role for every single activity they identified in the process.

To help people express process roles, a simple standard naming convention was used: process roles, like activities, would be named using a verb and a noun. Thus, the water engineer role in a "Design water network" process would, for example, simply be called "Calculate network load", the plumber's role in a "Maintain water network" process would be called "Install water network", the CEO's process role in a "Procurement" process would be called "Approve negotiated price".

Thinking of process roles and expressing them like this changes people's perspective about their jobs: **one realizes that we all play different roles in different processes. Summing up one person's roles constitutes that person's Job Description. That was an eye-opener for the majority of people involved in the Project.**

Deliverables: What Gets Provided When All the Work is Done?

Whether it is a product or a service, every process delivers something to someone. A deliverable could be thought of as the container of the value requested by the one who triggered the process.

Every time one process role handed over its work to the next process role in line, it also involved a deliverable: what one process role expects from the previous process role in order to be able to do his/her job. These intermediary deliverables actually represent the lowest level of responsibility within an organization. Properly naming them is a good exercise to clarify responsibility for each process role in a process. This also helps people understand that the output of their process role is further used by the next process role and so on until getting to the final process deliverable. All their contributions combine into what the stakeholder asked for.

Because Apa Nova wanted to strengthen responsibility at all levels, process roles would be mapped together with their deliverables, so that each employee could understand exactly what he/she needed to do and what he/she was responsible to provide. Deliverables would also have a simple naming convention within the Project. They would be formulated as nouns, the same noun as used within the name of the process role, followed by their status (provided by the action verb used to describe the activity preceding the deliverable). For example, the process role "Approve negotiated price" generates a deliverable called "Negotiated price approved".

From-To: Where Does the Process Come From and Where Does It Go?

Another simple request at the beginning of the Project was to document where a process or process fragment comes from (who triggers it), and where it goes to (who is the recipient of the deliverable). This simple request was in fact the linchpin for everyone involved to create the Process Architecture. It provided the necessary information to see where process fragments should connect, and to know when processes had finally been properly identified. As fragmented as the processes might have been, any presentation of any fragment would start with the key links needed at the beginning and at the end, in order to assemble the entire process.

With this simple conceptual framework, the scene had been set to identify Apa Nova's processes, starting from the bottom and working our way up.

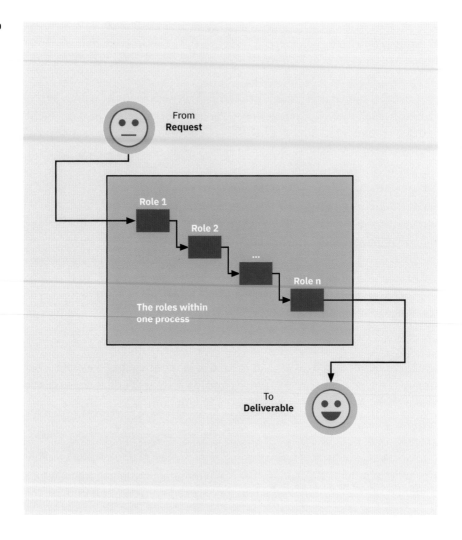

All Fragments of Work – the Excruciating Effort of Putting It All on Paper

It was time to get an image of the work done at Apa Nova. All types of work. In every department, by every type of worker. Every activity, every role, every approval, every send-off and registration of every paper. Everything!

At first, the Project teams in Apa Nova were responsible for mapping the work they did within their department – Process Fragments – and then for presenting them to other teams in weekly review meetings. This gave everyone the chance to see what the others were working on, thus sharing enough details so that later they could piece the fragments together into processes.

For example, the first meeting with the Project team from the Metering department took place on the 18th of January, 2016, in one of their offices, later in the day, after everyone had finished with daily chores and pressing activities. Like all new beginnings, it was a learning journey for all: slowly getting to know each other, understanding why we were all there, gaining trust and beginning our actual task. For such a meeting to be successful, it must be treated like a well-choreographed dance. It requires presence and attention from all participants, for all to move in sync and let themselves be guided into an exploratory journey of capturing knowledge. It requires well-crafted questions to get the team going. Imagine you are part of the team:

- What are your processes?
- What is required of you?
- What are your roles in the processes?
- What do you do all day long?
- What is the first activity in the process?
- Who does what?
- What gets you working on something?

It's important to ask as many follow-up questions from as many angles as possible to be sure everything gets documented according to day-to-day reality. But people seldom remember in a flash all the activities they perform and, in most cases, the way one person describes these activities isn't the way someone else understands them.

So real mapping sessions became a monumental exercise in communication and understanding. They created, through shared experiences and human interaction, a common understanding of the work everyone does. In hindsight, this was likely the main purpose of the mapping sessions.

For 78 days in a row, including weekends, if you walked into any meeting room in the company offices scattered around Bucharest, you'd have found Project teams buzzing over process maps of the work done in their department. It was a massive effort with people working after hours and even during weekends. Each of the 22 Project teams strived tirelessly to map and document their own process fragments – what entered their area of responsibility up until their job was done and passed towards another structure within the organization. Review, map, review, feedback, map, repeat.

*A first attempt at identifying processes in the Metering department –
more than 100 process fragments identified*

All of this effort taken by all the Project teams, generated many pieces of process maps, in some departments several dozens, in others even hundreds; all in all, more than 1 500 fragments. Now it was time to piece together the puzzle, uncovering the image of work within the company.

Piecing It All Together

The key outcome of this phase was to assemble the processes of the organization. While seemingly a straightforward proposition with apparently no technical difficulty, it proved to be the single most transformative element of the Reengineering Project.

A process must have an internal or external customer. Then, it must have a start and an end. Finally, it has a series of activities that span in one or more departments or functional units. In theory, this sounds really straightforward. But practice can sometimes be more interesting than theory.

If you ask a few hundred people to work with this explanation, you will soon find that they cannot agree on key aspects of the processes. Chief amongst these practical dilemmas are the process start and end. Ask two teams to specify where the process starts and where it ends, and you will get two, or even three different answers.

This became painfully clear to the top management team after the first reviews of process fragments, while testing to see how fast process assembly would go down the road. One of them stated: *"We seem to be unable to write down what we do! You only need to look at these maps and it's obvious: the processes have no end and no beginning."*

Of course, this is only one of the crucial pitfalls to overcome in a successful effort of transformation. Thus, a more down-to-earth definition of a process was gradually introduced: **everything that must happen as a consequence of a stakeholder's request to the satisfaction of that request**.

Preparing for the inevitable questions, a corollary of that definition came in handy, considering the high degree of process fragmentation in the company: **processes are truly discovered within the organization when all the fragments (i.e. activities) that serve the initial request have been pieced together**. Equipped with this definition, the teams could continue piecing the company's processes together. After each team had worked separately, they had to meet and present to each other what they achieved.

The weekly review meetings were the perfect opportunity to do just that. They were time-consuming, most of them taking full days out of many people's schedules. Everyone presented their progress, everyone commented, tried to understand and offered feedback to all those involved.

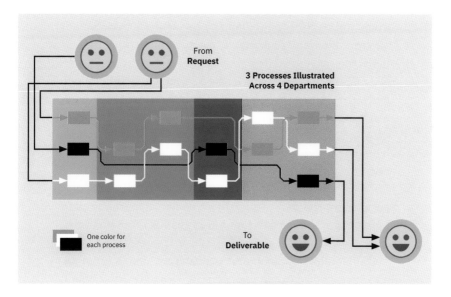

Bottom-Up Process Discovery

The Willingness to Join Hands and Keep Them Together

As processes were painstakingly assembled, the Project teams were asked to keep documentation up to date. That meant physically and digitally stitching process maps together – it would have been a simple task, were it not for an understandable phenomenon described in a few stories below:

- After an assembly meeting, one of the participants literally reported: *"We went there with open arms and to join hands, and in return we got some feet"* (in Romanian, the latter phrase literally means "to get kicked"). They went there to work together and not only did they leave empty-handed, but their co-workers had also turned the meeting into a complaining assembly, laying the blame for all their difficulties on everyone else;
- At the end of some of the meetings with multiple departments working on the same process, the same questions kept popping up: *"Should I include my document into yours, or should you include your document into mine? Who should take care of the process map until the next meeting?"* It would frequently happen that two Project teams left a meeting with the verbal agreement that one would integrate the other's fragment into their map and, at the beginning of the next meeting, each Project team would still be holding on to their fragment of the process map;
- At one of the weekly reviews, a team was presenting the status of the assembled processes. Being one of the most zealous and productive teams in the Project, its members had made the effort to read the other team's process fragment maps in advance, and found some that could be integrated with their fragments. So, they decided to quickly take action, but didn't inform anyone from the other team. The presentation progressed quite well until the Q&A Session. A member of the other team stood up, and while pointing at the previous speaker, proclaimed, *"They stole our process."* Apparently, they were unhappy about someone joining hands without permission. Doesn't all of this sound familiar? Please keep in mind that all of these reactions are somehow justified – done well and open-heartedly, process maps are a symbol of people's work and some people identify profoundly with their work. As pieces of work are stitched together, going back and forth

across departments, the key question is actually *"who should*
take care of our work?" This happens due to the fragmentation of
management combined with the fragmentation of work, and it
is the main cause of so much of what ails organizations today.
A few weeks into process assembly, someone became quite
vocal about it, stating: *"I think we are all too tired of giving and
getting process fragments back and forth."*

One of the participants suggested that, just like a baby needs a parent until it
grows up, so do the processes as they are being assembled. Everybody loved
the analogy. From then on, the question became *"who wants to be the parent of
this process?"* It humanized the process and made it seem like a fragile being in
need of care and attention. At that point in the Project, it really was. The word
"parent" managed to imply certain status and responsibility and, most importantly, it worked. Afterwards, people were joking in meetings about how many
kids (processes) they had, but they also agreed more easily to have someone
integrate the process fragments. That was the seed of process ownership. It
would later become the basic responsibility of the process owner, as will be
further described in the following sections.

During reviews, it became clear that some of the processes presented
were not yet fully assembled, but remained, rather, a collection of process fragments. Asked about the progress of the assembly effort, the team leader from
one department answered: *"We stitched together the 105 process fragments into 23
processes, and we are the parents of two of these. The other 21 are still orphans."*

Each one of the 22 Project teams interacted in multiple ways with each
other, like a crazy dance of musical chairs. Sometimes the dance was excru-
ciating: imagine 7 representatives from 7 departments standing up to present a piece of work, then sitting right back down after handing the work to
another teammate, all in all more than 25 times across a single process. It felt
physically tiring and a bit confusing. After finishing one significantly large
process (87 roles over 15 structures) someone exclaimed: *"This time we joined
hands, next time we should just hug each other."*

It was a learning experience for everyone involved, sensitive for some, uplifting for others. It was truly a humbling experience to witness the variety of ways in which people reacted when actually trying to piece together a process out of the myriad of fragments, from start to end. But witnessing it over and over again revealed the true scope of the fragmentation in the company.

Project teams, which at that point were structure-based and represented process fragments, were dissolved and reassembled into actual process teams, according to the processes that had been pieced together, and their "parents". **This helped the company to steadily move away from siloed thinking towards process thinking.**

During cross-function meetings like these, people spoke openly about the issues they had with their co-workers from different functions and departments, for the very first time. They worked their brains out, raised specific topics and addressed old work situations.

Naming What We Do

As processes were being assembled, the teams needed to state what they were working on and to present their work. This proved harder than expected because people named processes in a specific way, depending on their perspective or on historical names like "the shuttle file" meaning "Close contract". As the top management team started to push for proper names, people pushed back with the obvious question: *"How should processes be named?"* The answer was: *"It depends where the process starts and where it ends"* – and the members of the top management team got very much involved, enforcing the empowerment credo they had put in place at the start of the Project, and also allowing people the space to really think about the true scope of each process. On top of this, they also asked for the implementation of a simple naming convention: just like activities, process roles and process fragments before, process names would be formed as: Verb + Noun. Thus, the correct name would be "Close contract" instead of "Contracts", and "Fix water network fault" instead of "Faults".

Slowly, the processes of Apa Nova began to unfold. Filling up the walls of the review rooms, some processes would stretch for 10–15 feet on A4 paper sheets taped together. The mystery was solved and it impressed everyone. The number of processes that emerged was almost ten times smaller than the number of process fragments. People stared at these papers and, for the first time, they saw all the processes of the company. Many insisted on pointing out: *"It all finally makes sense now."*

With each process they understood, everyone saw their work in a new light, and could place it inside the bigger picture and in relation to the needs of external stakeholders. **The feeling was that the organization became manageable as a whole.** As one of the members of the Design department put it: *"Now, for the first time, I can understand every step that we take together. And once there is visibility and transparency, you can plainly see what is useful. It's the first time in my career that I have a picture of everything, from the water catchments to the sewage water treatment."*

D. Process Grouping

Why Should We Group Processes?

Process identification, as seen so far, enables everyone to look beyond the small activities run in different departments in order to see what every employee actually does for every stakeholder. It gets an organization out of the fragmentation trap and into seeing the end results. But a list of, say, 150 properly identified processes is just not enough to properly manage a company. Some processes are closely linked to others (for example, all processes related to a specific stakeholder are linked to each other), while some seem to be very loosely related to one another (for example, "Provide water" and "Evaluate personnel performance").

One realizes the need to organize the processes so as to be able to better manage them. So, how should processes be organized? This is exactly what the top management team of Apa Nova asked Advanced Thinking, as the processes were identified.

Process Groups – How Processes Should Be Grouped and Managed
The key criteria for process grouping had been given by Advanced Thinking and discussed with the top management team from the very beginning: **Stakeholders Identification**. Would it not make a lot of sense to take all the processes that are generated by, say, the customer's needs, and look at them together? This gives a new meaning to concepts like the relationship with the customer, as it translates from a process group perspective into *"all the things we do (processes) to address the customer's needs."*

Even in their assembled form, the amount of processes in a large company is impressive. On a first count, Apa Nova had more than 100. People were introduced to the principle explained above and, as soon as they understood it, they displayed strong emotional reactions. *"That means that all of the company's processes are under the customer-related process group"*, exclaimed one team-member during a review meeting. Even if most people in a company work within customer-related processes, it is natural that not all processes are customer-triggered.

Food for thought:

- How many processes do we really have?
- Who triggers them and where do they end?
- How can we organize everything we need to do so as to answer all of our stakeholders' needs?
- How can we re-imagine the process in order to make a significant improvement for its stakeholders?

3. Rethinking How We Do Business: Process Reengineering

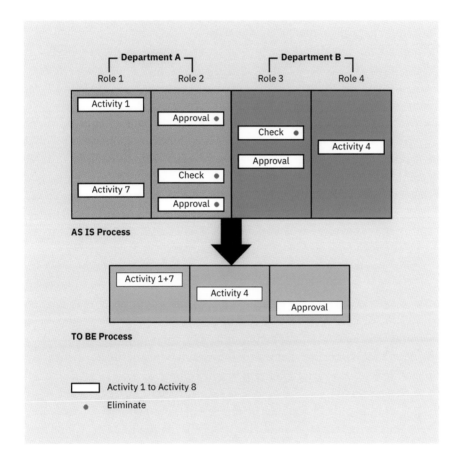

With the complete list of processes literally on the walls, everyone could begin reinventing their organization.

Everybody had been congratulated for their tremendous effort to assemble the processes, but at this point, they were basically asked to review all of that work again. And they continued to do it together, as Project teams. The new way of doing business was all up to the people.

This too, did not start without pushback. The most frequent question was: *"Why do we need to change anyway?"* This would be followed by all sorts of arguments, ranging from *"we are used to doing things this way, won't it be less efficient if we change?"* all the way to *"it's not like people can get their drinking water from someone other than us."* The Project management team had to remind everyone about the initial need for change and the reasons for doing this significant Transformation.

Permission to Change: Rethinking Apa Nova

Rethinking the way things are done is not something people are used to. It takes patience and constant communication from the top management team, including to explicitly give permission to change. In Apa Nova's organizational culture, people were used to accepting orders without question and executed them to the best of their abilities, in spite of other priorities or ongoing work.

Take, for example, one specific review meeting, where someone proposed that middle managers had to formulate better requirements for specific development projects, according to the quality standards that the Project team had designed. The proposal was made in a timid voice. When asked why this is a significant change, one of the members of the Project team had to explain that, in the past, the process had been guided by conflicting directives, coming from different managers – all of whom were in the room.

"It is your right not to accept everything we say, we might sometimes be wrong. We need you to challenge us!" exclaimed one of the members of the top management team. People in the group began smiling and someone mustered the courage to ask: *"Are you sure?"* Several other top managers answered *"Yes!"* Many review meetings were spent trying to empower people in this way.

This process-related dialogue was the foundation of the Reengineering Project. Three main vectors were guiding this effort:

1. **Creating the Process Architecture** – gaining a strong understanding of how different processes work together, as described in the previous section of this chapter;
2. **First Pass Simplification** of the existing processes – eliminating redundancies and bureaucracy;
3. **Process Innovation**, anywhere it was truly needed at this moment in the Project.

First Pass Simplification

Every organization comes to a point where it needs to simplify its operations. But simplification is often misunderstood and the real-life projects that follow in practice are often disappointing. They either end up being Technology/IT implementation projects, or small cleaning projects done one process at a time, with too few real-life benefits.

Apa Nova set out on this path with an ambitious vision: the entire company was in line for a genuine simplification – making all processes easier to execute – and the solutions would have to speak for themselves, pen to paper. The effort would be done by everyone, within every process, and it would create a robust foundation for data-driven Continuous Improvement in the future. To add to this tall order, non-performing processes that generated problems for the company would have to be addressed as a matter of priority.

The Project teams were introduced to basic process clean-up concepts like value-added versus non value-added activities, eliminating redundancies, 7 Wastes, simple 5S principles, and they quickly started to review each process, looking for opportunities to improve them. Reviews turned into debates on different process improvement ideas.

Slowly, people started bringing in data to prove process issues and the conversation really heated up. The top management team members quickly realized that, this way, they could actually rise above day-to-day issues, facilitating a conversation about how things could work better. The dialogue changed from naming and blaming, to "what is the best idea for this process?" What used to be orders (reflecting only what one manager thought of as the best solution) became suggestions for process teams to go beyond current limits, and phrases like *"I think we should keep thinking about this process in which we seem to have previously tangled"* became the norm.

By far the most frequent improvement actions proposed by Project teams were the redesign of process roles by merging small process roles into one, and reducing the number of hand-offs by simply re-ordering process activities to flow smoother.

Another type of improvement that took on the status of a mantra was the elimination of successive approvals. Once the processes had been assembled, it became clear to everyone that almost every hand-off in the process between two departments was historically marked by a manager's approval, going out of department A and entering department B. So, the process flow was always restricted or delayed by approvals when transitioning from one structure to the next.

Realizing the considerable waste of time this entailed, the top management team insisted relentlessly for all these approvals to be eliminated, "pushing" responsibility down to the right level – the lowest organizational level possible. The blowback of eliminating approvals came quickly: what would managers do if all the time spent signing papers was going to be eliminated?

When asked if they wanted to sign all those approvals, most of them said they neither needed to, nor enjoyed it, but it was just the way things were done, because people asked to "cover" their work with a manager's signature. It was also explained that a manager's job in a modern organization should go far beyond such mundane tasks, and into resourcing the process, monitoring it in the right way, adjusting it at its core – not correcting the mistakes of his/her employees. Envisioning their work in this way and understanding how much of their time would be saved made them let go of all the bureaucracy and let the processes flow.

The overall impact in process role reduction throughout the Project was significant. The number of process roles in the TO BE processes dropped on average by 27.6% and the number of hand-offs was reduced by more than half of the initial count.

Seeing the processes end-to-end for the first time inspired another kind of improvement concerning redundancies and the grey areas in the organization. Apart from just finding endless approvals in processes, the teams also realized there were significant pieces of value-added activities, such as analyses and decisions, data processing, etc. that were being done more than once within a process.

Each of them also came with subsequent checks and verifications – "just to be sure" – meaning that they would take place more than once without ever changing the final output of the process. These overlaps did not happen because people enjoyed doing them or considered them a critical part of their job, but because they were rather historical process overlaps that evolved in time, and process roles were not clear. **All this had been taken on as common practice, and, as a result, structures had a life of their own.** Project teams quickly decided to eliminate them to make processes more efficient.

This "just to be sure" kind of thinking also tends to apply to processes. Project teams found instances of reporting processes that had not been needed in more than 3 years, but were still active. Even more, in some cases, processes were quite thorough and labor-intensive because measurement was not automated, and people were collecting data by hand, unnecessarily.

Within other processes, Project teams found missing process fragments: points in the process where it was not clear who was responsible to continue the work and how. Usually, people called this activity "provide point of view". For instance, within the "Provide contract" process, the person responsible for

a particular case would sometimes write an email to a list of 7 or more recipient departments like Legal, Technical, the 6 Sectorial Operations departments, Archiving and Environmental Protection, titled "Please provide point
of view", and a list of documents attached. Looking at the replies one could see
that some departments had never answered – apparently, they felt no need
to provide their opinion – while others had conflicting opinions, leaving the
person responsible for the case confused and unable to move forward with
the contract.

Within a series of meetings, it became obvious to everyone that, to create
the TO BE state of this process, it was again necessary to identify the missing
roles. It wasn't clear what the person in charge of a customer's case needed from
everyone in the distribution list, and if their opinions were actually necessary.
As a result, in some instances, the points of view offered by one department
overstepped another department's attributions.

In other cases, the requested points of view never came. Clear process
roles were paramount to provide exactly what the process needed, in the right
sequence. This is exactly what one of the Project teams created. The end result
was a contracting process that had a standard backbone and a few necessary
process variants, with clear rules for special cases when specific expertise
was needed.

One of the most important examples of grey area was the top management team discovering that processes were missing altogether. Sometimes,
this happened because teams had simply forgotten to map a process. During
one of the review meetings, a member of the top management team asked one
of the Project team leaders why the process is missing and implied that maybe
it is not executed in real life. The Project team leader instantly became aggra-
vated and replied: *"Asking me if we do this is like asking me if I am breathing!"* – it
was obvious that the activity was so self-evident to him that he did not even
feel it was worth mapping!

Other times, processes were missing because certain requirements had
only been stated on a business level but never became operationalized. One
such example was found in the Human Resources department, where there had
been a long-standing request to create career plans for employees and, while
management expected it, in effect there was no actual process for it because
nobody had the know-how. In such cases, teams simply created processes
together from scratch.

Process Innovation

Some processes went beyond simplification, and they were completely redesigned. This was the case of the "Repair water faults" process. First of all, the AS IS version of the process was actually comprised of 6 different variations of the same process. This was because Apa Nova's Operational departments – the ones handling the technical part of this process – had been historically split into six geographical Sectors, mirroring the administrative organization of the City of Bucharest. As one member of the top management team explained: *"There was a time in the history of Apa Nova when we split into 6 Sectors because each Sector Mayor of Bucharest wanted to have his own little Apa Nova to play with."*

In practice, this generated peculiar behaviors: if you were a customer calling Apa Nova's call center from an address at the geographical delimitation of two Sectors in Bucharest, you might have an Apa Nova crew available across the street and because it was not assigned to your sector, you would end up waiting for hours for another crew to be assigned to fix the fault in your water network. Of course, this geographical fragmentation had also generated six different versions of the same processes, each managed by a different Sector manager in his own way, having his own version of an Organizational Structure.

It also meant that each Sector had slightly different technologies to work with and an unbalanced allocation of resources – some Sectors had less faults to handle but more resources than the rest, and other Sectors had more faults with less resources – which obviously created a much longer waiting time for customers in some Sectors than others, frustrated employees and heated arguments, and generated fierce competition between managers. All of that had a negative impact on the company.

In creating the TO BE version of those processes, the priority was to obtain ONE version – the best one, integrating the best knowledge gained from the different experiences of all six teams. This also meant applying the "local action – global control" principle. Enabled by information technology, network maintenance crews would work just like taxi drivers – an available crew, closest to the fault, would immediately pick-up the case and head to the location for initial diagnostic.

The second redesign principle had to do with resource optimization and was enabled by better data understanding: historical data was analyzed, and it was discovered that more than 65% of customer reported faults were solvable on the spot, not requiring digging equipment, or heavy parts. This meant that a different type of crew could be allocated to respond to customer complaints with smaller cars, less personnel, and available standard parts: quick response teams, as they were called. It translated into more than two thirds of the faults being resolved almost nine times faster, while keeping quality the same and lowering operational costs.

In the few cases when these quick-response teams could not address the issue – they needed digging machinery, special parts, etc. – they would still help the process move faster. They would pinpoint the fault, contain the area to protect citizens, make room for the second-tier team, collect the necessary information for the prioritization of the large fault and relay it to the second team. It's just like when a triage doctor in the emergency room establishes priorities and sends critical patients to specialized doctors after they had been stabilized. Then the quick-response team would just move on to the next fault – as needed – and the second team would come in, ready to start fixing, like a surgeon whose patients had been prepped.

The Project team also saw this as an opportunity to enhance the relationship with the customer. If water services would have to be shut down temporarily for a large repair, all the customers affected by the intervention would receive notifications before the water services would be shut down, including an estimated time for service recovery. For sensitive customers, like schools, hospitals, etc., a special version of the process implied that customers would give explicit approval or reschedule the intervention before it could move further. Overall, a fundamental rethinking of the process had been achieved with dramatic improvements across all KPIs – Quality, Cost and Delivery Time – a textbook example of a Reengineering Project.

When building a house, you first have to create a solid foundation. In the case of Apa Nova, as in any other serious business transformation project, that foundation is Process Architecture. People had designed their processes, now it was time to execute them, to forget the old practices, to determine themselves to trust the "new" – since the "new" was the collaborative result of their thoughts, ideas and creative solutions to building better processes.

After all the reengineering efforts across all process groups, Apa Nova can account for a 27.6% reduction in the total number of process roles, a 52% reduction in hand-offs between process roles, reducing time between steps and opportunities for error, and a 23% reduction in reworking loops across all its processes – adding up to hundreds of iterations.

The overall results of all this rethinking were dramatic: creating more straightforward processes all around, and a simpler responsibility role-based matrix for work. This was achieved even though the implementation of Lean and other Improvement Methodologies was not the focus of this phase in the

Reengineering Project, as lean-type results are still to be expected from a **well implemented Business Transformation Project.**

4. An Organizational Structure that Supports Processes

Eliminating the Silo, Creating a Structure that Works

In the light of the previous sections, it should be doubtless by now that Process Architecture (i.e. process identification and their translation into process groups) is fundamental to competitive corporate success. Every organizational element links back to the Process Architecture. The same should be true of the Organizational Structure.

In this frame, the redesign of the Organizational Structure emerges from Process Architecture and not vice versa. It reflects the responsibilities of the company to fulfill all of their stakeholders' expectations, instead of the traditional view of a chain of command and control that impedes the flow of the process by fragmenting it and placing artificial organizational boundaries within it. This is quite a paradigm shift that moves the focus of management from different entitlements of various organizational positions in a fragmented structure (i.e. suboptimization) to the entitlement of the entire process.

You may wonder what kind of Organizational Structure design criteria can lead to such changes. Well, the present section aims to answer this question for you.

At the beginning of the redesign phase of the Organizational Structure, Apa Nova was not an exception from the traditional perspective. Its structure was trapped in schemes and charts. It created the impression that it could be arbitrarily modeled and remodeled when changes occurred. As people said during the meetings, past **restructuring attempts** only created the illusion of progress. More than that, Apa Nova's structure had eleven hierarchical levels. Eleven! It was complicated, unmanageable and incomprehensible, as even the newly appointed CEO had described it.

When asked whom a customer talks to when facing an issue, there were several answers: some mentioned the Call Center, others the Production Department, or the Front Office, and so on. You may be wondering: what was the issue with those different answers? If you already know what the problem was, and if this knowledge comes from an effort of business transformation, let us sincerely congratulate you. It means you already went through the roller

coaster of every aspect related to it and you can understand, indeed, the feelings and efforts that paved the road in that direction. If you do not know it, the
roller coaster begins for you as it started for Apa Nova four years ago. When
analyzing these answers, two main arguments became evident:

First, those were the names of departments that dealt with different fragments of customer-related issues in isolation, providing fragmented, sometimes contradictory solutions within a narrow management frame.

Second, these answers assume that customers should be aware of how
the company is organized internally in order to know where to address their
enquiry. Is this what should primarily matter in relation to any stakeholder
(customers being one of the stakeholders)? Of course not.

Let's look at the picture below:

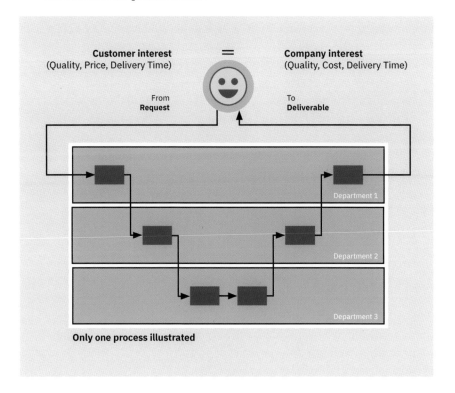

Customer interest = **Company interest**
(Quality, Price, Delivery Time) (Quality, Cost, Delivery Time)

From To
Request **Deliverable**

Department 1

Department 2

Department 3

Only one process illustrated

The picture made it obvious: both the company's and the stakeholders' (including customers) interests were the same at the end of any given process, and
not in any one of the individual departments. In other words, none of the company's stakeholders has an interest in the internal standardized procedures

of an organization. Their only interest is in the fulfillment of their needs and expectations at the end of the processes they trigger. And surprisingly, this holds true for the company as well.

As it was described in the previous sections, process groups are generated by stakeholders at company level and consist of all the identified processes that relate to those stakeholders.

Thus, the significance of departments became questionable and generated a learning experience of how to filter out the important things from the less important, the sound from the noise. But these tough realizations only strengthened the sense of engagement, which allowed to further explore the subtleties of the Organizational Structure redesign.

The picture above also sheds light on something else: it was not just about managing from the wrong (departmental) level, but also with the wrong scoping: the processes often exceeded departmental limits. When asked who is literally responsible for the entire process – i.e. who is responsible for the customer's and the company's interest in that process – people hesitated to answer.

In fact, it was "NOBODY", as the management team had realized in their first workshop. This observation added more complexity to the discussions and shook up the existent beliefs and management practices like an earthquake. Many of the perspectives about how to manage a business successfully had been pushed beyond their limits. It was one of the many moments that unwillingly touched the egos in the room.

Generally, such revelations have a powerful impact on conventional management practices and are always difficult to accept. And once accepted, they are only halfway in the Organizational Structure design process, marking the completion of its awareness-building phase.

Accepting the idea is one thing, putting it into practice is even more difficult. As time went by and there was enough understanding within the Project to make a process-driven Organizational Structure a reality, there were new difficulties coming up. While one member of the top management team of Apa Nova considered naming people as official process owners, he realized that this would imply selecting a different kind of person than traditionally promoted in management positions.

Let's take an example from a customer-triggered process, "Provide installation approval". The purpose of this process is to assure a potential customer that there is at least one viable technical solution for him/her to link to a public – water, sewage, gas, electrical, etc. – utility from his property, considering all the physical constraints of the land, its placement in the urban context, all of the other utilities providers and the legal constraints placed by public building standards.

Mapping the process across the existing departmental Organizational Structure revealed that it went through the Customer Relations department, the Operational department, the Technical department, the Operational Coordination department, the Production department, the Legal department and the Archiving department – 7 structures at the N-2 level. When trying to place this entire process under one responsibility, it becomes clear that the person overseeing the process simply can't be a specialized practitioner of any of the disciplines necessary within the process, but rather a facilitator of them all – a true manager, able to work across the traditional boundaries and align objectives between everybody involved.

Another example that reveals a case of aligning the structure to the process is the "Hire personnel" process: it can start off in any existing structure within the organization – as anyone can request new hires – and it goes through the Human Resources department, sometimes "outside" the organization, then back "in" for the validation of the new hire, through the EHS department, back to HR and it ends where it started. Placing this process under one responsibility means having someone align every part of the process, including the way in which requests for new hires are done and how the way onboarding and initial EHS training is delivered.

In both of these examples (and in any other correctly identified process across the organization), Advanced Thinking proposed that process ownership should be attributed to the right Organizational Structures: the structure that first receives the request, at company level, should be the structure with process ownership – as it is the first to come in contact with the stakeholder of the process and, in most cases, the last to face that stakeholder in providing him/her with the deliverable of the process.

On top of naming process owners, a clear description of this role was put forward to clarify its authority and responsibility, focusing on the setting of targets and evaluation, standardization, Risk Management, and Continuous Improvement. This was done to make sure there is "end-to-end" process responsibility in the new Organizational Structure, at some level.

This would work even if the organization was not fully ready to be process-based in the beginning, but rather process-driven. In this intermediary phase, process owners would start, for the first time in the company's history, to see the way everything links together and to align processes, as the new organizational infrastructure was completed.

In later phases, as the new KPI infrastructure would provide full visibility of the link between process performance and process resources, a second iteration of the structure could be put into place, entirely process-based.

Another future development of the Organizational Structure would follow the optimization of process groups. This means making the final links between processes within a process group, and between the process groups themselves. It was decided to accomplish this final Process Architecture only after the Alignment & Standardization of processes within all the Veolia companies in Romania in order to take advantage of all the synergies that would emerge as result (see Chapter 4).

Moving on with the Organizational Structure redesign process, here is another question: how does an Organizational Structure emerge from the Process Architecture created out of the identified processes?

The process group generated by the stakeholder "Customer" at company level contained nine identified customer-related processes. The next step was to decide how this process group would be organized on optimum responsibility levels in the new Organizational Structure, to facilitate the creation of business management value. It was a bidirectional decision-making process in which top-down decisions met bottom-up knowledge.

Employees were given time to debate and were empowered to take decisions. In return, they were expected to deliver a serious opinion about what they saw as the most critical processes to take up to the next responsibility level, until the integration of all processes in the group could be achieved. The principles that guided this construction were based on the concept of ownership over the process group, as well as the process.

The redesigned Organizational Structure is a significantly evolved phase in management practices, representing a new and simple Framework for Management Responsibility. It enables a more integrated management of processes, built on a stakeholder and process logic. It is also much flatter and suppler than the company's initial structure, going from 11 to 6 levels of responsibility. As one member of the management team said, *"If I had known about all of this ten or twenty years ago, I would be in a different place today."*

Today, the Organizational Structure within Apa Nova is undergoing its second review, fully integrating the notion of process owner with a process group logic that will simplify the structure even more. It will also implement higher level organizational principles, which will tightly connect it with the overall country business architecture within Veolia (more on this in Chapter 4).

5. From an Opinion-Based Management to Data-Driven Management: The Stakeholder-Driven KPI Architecture

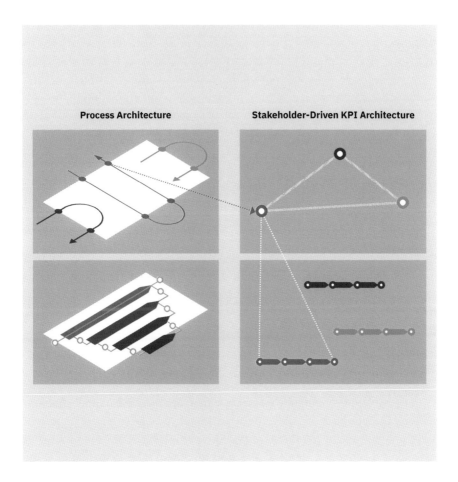

A. An Industry Defined by High Standards of Quality

It's important to have a straightforward understanding of a performance indicator: it's a quantifiable metric that measures any type of performance, and it is composed of a name, a definition, a clear measurement method, and a unit of measurement.

In the water utilities sector, providing drinking water for the population is crucial. Public health and safety are the first priority for every company in this sector, and authorities carefully oversee every step of this process. Apa

Nova always had extensive metrics for the quality of the water produced. In any organization, and especially in this one, one will always find areas in which good metrics and performance indicators already exist. Some areas will always be better measured than others.

It's no news to anyone experienced in the management of an organization that piles of low-quality data could lurk in the most unexpected places. Apa Nova was no different than most. A lot of metrics and performance indicators were measured and reported upon. Yearly, monthly, weekly, daily and, at times, hourly reports contained unreliable data. Sometimes, there was conflicting information in two different reports from two different departments. Furthermore, even if many reports were created, key data was missing. All this meant they failed to provide any real insight for better decision-making.

Having said all this, you may want to think about the following:

1. How many performance indicators are enough for an organization?
2. How do you know that they are the right ones?

The journey of setting up the KPI Architecture and a dashboard to match it didn't start from scratch at Apa Nova. After the identification of the metrics already in use, they had to analyze which ones would be kept, which ones would be improved and what needed to be designed altogether. For this, all employees from all levels of the organization were involved in identifying and designing all the relevant KPIs to properly run the business. This will be gradually implemented during the Continuous Improvement phase.

Picture an aircraft. Nowadays, planes enable people to travel at previously unimaginable speeds across continents and oceans, to reach their destination. So, for it to reach its destination, the aircraft itself must be operated at the right time, under the right conditions and at affordable costs. A team of professionals makes this happen. Some fly the aircraft, others cater to the needs of the passengers, all at the same time. Their process roles are clear, the processes they work in are optimized for both effectiveness and efficiency. Effectively, flying the aircraft is a 6 Sigma process with little room for error, either technical, human or otherwise. Errors within such a process lead to catastrophic consequences. But here comes a question: how does the team know, every second of every flight, that what they are doing is flawless? How do they control this marvelous piece of technology and how do they measure the success of their work?

The answer is that they have the cockpit – a part of the plane, designed especially for the pilot and its crew, a place that contains all the instruments and controls in order to successfully pilot the plane. Do you think the layout of the cockpit was randomly assembled? No. Of course there was a plan behind it. Behind every gauge and every switch, there was certainly a complex thought process. While the passenger's request is to safely, comfortably and timely reach his/her destination – the cockpit displays flight controls and information about the navigation, flight performance, communication instruments, and so on. All the information in the cockpit is a display of customer demands (safely, comfortably, timely), translated into measurable metrics, to be satisfied. These metrics are gathered from within the processes.

That is what Apa Nova wanted: a "cockpit" to help manage and lead the organization towards reaching its goals. They wanted a dashboard that showed significant metrics, which mirrored all the processes and all the work being done, all linked together at the highest levels of Key Performance Indicators. Apa Nova set out to implement a KPI Architecture capable of providing real-time feedback of the processes, which would enable the company to make faster and better decisions.

Once an organization identifies its processes, it's crucial to get a crystal clear picture of how to measure their success. Apa Nova needed an accurate translation of its stakeholders' needs into measurable and controllable metrics provided by the processes, starting with the shop floor – where work is being done, where outputs are created from inputs.

B. Measuring Success: Process Performance Indicators

The process of designing KPIs begins by correctly linking the request that triggers the process with the successful delivery of that request. That means correctly assessing what satisfies the stakeholder once the stakeholder receives the output. Engaging employees from every level within the organization leads to exactly that! For each and every process within the organization! An intricate, but essential job, isn't it?

Regardless of the process or its purpose, delivering a product or service, its final output – the deliverable – can be evaluated based on three characteristics: Quality, Cost and Delivery Time. **At the end of the day, all "other" aspects like EHS, Employee Morale, etc. are quality aspects, just coming from a different stakeholder.** How good is that product or service in terms of quality? How much did it cost to make? How much time did it take for it to reach the customer? These were the leading questions guiding Apa Nova in deciding what and how to measure the success of their processes.

As mentioned before, a process is triggered by a stakeholder's expressed request. It can be a simple request such as a new hire or a request for information from a call center. A process performs well if the final deliverable matches the stakeholder's expectations. That simple!

If a customer is calling to inquire about his bill and he gets his answer fast and accurately, he/she will consider the experience as valuable. His requirements will have been met. The process designed to answer to his/her request performed accordingly. At the end of this process, in terms of quality (of the information provided) and time taken to provide the information, success will have been achieved. So, you can count another happy customer!

Like any other company, Apa Nova has to close contracts with its customers, so a closed contract is, in this case, the business object. What's important to measure, in the end? What represents quality? How much does it cost to execute the process from the moment a customer places a request until the contract is signed? How long does it take? The process of providing water is measured from all three perspectives (Quality, Cost and Delivery Time). Once the measurements are compared to a target, you can correctly assess if the process is successful or not.

Consider you have accurately captured the "voice" of your stakeholder (his/her requests) and translated it into measurable KPIs for your output. What would be the next natural step, so you can be sure that at every step, from the very first activity, you are on the right track towards success, towards meeting your stakeholder's expectations?

Earlier, we talked about the Project teams (consisting of Apa Nova's employees) who worked on KPIs. With the business object and the stakeholders' expectations in mind, they had to design KPIs that measured the fulfilment of those expectations.

For some stakeholders, it was already clear what needed to be achieved at the end of a process. There was no discussion about what it really meant to "Provide quality water" and how to measure that. Though, for other processes under analysis, there were some revelations along this journey. One occurred within the HR team. The process under discussion was "Hire new personnel."

The meeting was going smoothly. Around a large table in a perfectly lit room, everyone from the Recruitment department was looking at their mapped process, ready to work on setting up their KPIs. *"The process ends when the employment contract is signed by the newly selected recruit"*, everyone agreed. They concluded that their work was done. The process ended with a delivered business object, the signed employment contract, which had to be measured accordingly.

With that in mind, they went along and presented their work in the plenary meeting, where all the teams that worked on all the processes got to be challenged by their peers with the purpose of improving each other's work. It was at that meeting when one manager from the Production department stood up and asked the HR team: *"How come this process ends with a signed contract if what I really need and ask of your team is a new employee ready to take on his/her daily activities?"* A long pause followed. The room went silent, and one could feel the managers in the room agreeing with what had just been said. It was clear that the HR team felt exposed in the face of such a simple truth – the true voice of their internal customer hadn't even crossed their mind. It was that precise moment that led the whole HR team back to the drawing board, back to the beginning, to the process.

Designing a new organizational element can trigger changes that improve the previously designed organizational elements. In this case, the design of the KPIs improved the "Hire new personnel" process. Not taking into account what the managers really wanted from Recruitment led to improperly identifying and mapping the process, which created irrelevant KPIs. Addressing the question of what really represents the success of the process from the point of view of the one who requested it – the manager needing to fill an open position within his/her team – led to changing the end of the process to also embed a fragment related to actually preparing new employees to become operational at their new jobs.

One reason why the above situation often happens is the fact that boundaries are unclear and so responsibility isn't addressed in a proper way. There is a substantial difference between having responsibility over the signing of an employment contract and taking the responsibility over onboarding a new employee. The scope of the process changes, the ownership of the process might change, and resources, KPIs and all other elements that follow could also be altered.

The stakes are high, but when an honest and productive conversation takes place between all parties involved, real transformation happens in the benefit of the organization as a whole. Bottom line, this is another crucial practice that continues to improve collaboration between departments, to communicate and agree upon metrics, towards the final goal.

It is common practice for any large organization to invest a lot of resources into discovering the customer's needs, but when it comes to other stakeholders (usually internal ones such as management or employees), it is believed that their needs are already known. Only after a genuine conversation takes place, is this "undoubted and self-evident truth" demolished.

C. Horizontal and Vertical Alignment of KPIs

Measuring the final results, though, is not nearly enough. It's too late to fix anything if your plane has gone astray – it's not enough to know that something went wrong. It would be a strategic misstep to determine only at the end of your effort of satisfying your stakeholder that you have unfortunately failed.

If you are the process owner of one process, measuring the final result would not help you sleep better at night. You still lack the tools to know if, while executing the process, you are on the right track to satisfy your customer. For that to happen, a horizontal alignment of KPIs has to be done. So, the next step would be to align the entire process, to control it from start to finish, and in the right order: starting with the end in mind and moving towards the beginning.

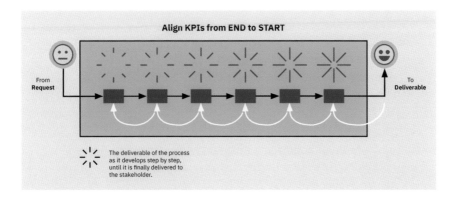

Align KPIs from END to START

From Request

To Deliverable

The deliverable of the process as it develops step by step, until it is finally delivered to the stakeholder.

When zooming into a process, one needs to design smart control points to be able to keep the end result in check. The best people for this job are always, without exception, the people working together within the process. The ones that intimately know the possible traps along the way of transforming inputs into outputs. That's exactly what happened at Apa Nova. The Project teams that had to design the proper KPIs at the end of the process had to continue their work within the process – and design the proper control points in the right places.

Once the team had a clear view of the process end and how to measure it, the next step was to agree on what should be controlled and at which point within the process, so as to reach the end result. Each role within the process, from the first one to the last, adds its value to the deliverable it receives and passes it over to the next role, until the business object is completed and delivered to the stakeholders. Each hand-off from one role to another is documented and formalized through a deliverable: the business object status at that point in the process. The Project teams' members needed to discuss things in depth and to reach an agreement so as to determine the Quality, Cost and Delivery Time metrics for each deliverable passing from one role to the other. In this way, everyone working within the process would know what they had to deliver for every step of the way, and at which standard of performance.

One of the most interesting examples of such a discussion emerged from a heated debate around the "Repair water and sewage network" process. Over 60% of the total costs of such a process came from fixing the pavement after the repair of the pipes. There was nothing to be done about these costs, since they were outsourced to external contractors and there was no getting around rebuilding the pavement. Moreover, these costs often exceeded the values estimated in the beginning of the process.

The team that was analyzing this process realized that the only way to reduce the overall cost was to reduce the actual area of intervention – this ended up being a key quality control point for three distinct roles: first, the one that has to pinpoint the exact fault location; the second, the one that would determine the area of intervention; the third, the one that would actually dig. These three roles would discover together an optimum digging area – thus, the related costs would be controlled. Accuracy of fault location, designated area of digging, and executed area of digging became critical process control points, each assigned to specific roles.

All KPIs that were defined at a process level were designed for and aligned between every process role. **That is what horizontal alignment means, at the lowest level of the company.**

The next challenge the team at Apa Nova had to solve was how to better consolidate these KPIs. Up until that moment, horizontal alignment had been a task for the Project teams to handle. Optimum upward consolidation required a thoroughly thought-out horizontal alignment of KPIs between processes.

Remember the airplane metaphor? When flying, customers know that they have to buy tickets beforehand, choose their seats, plan their luggage necessities, and select meal options long before the actual flight. They also have to check in. The information they must provide based on these decisions is an input for the luggage handling process in the airport, for the food serving process within the plane, and so on. The process of buying a plane ticket is aligned with the ones that follow. Properly performed, they altogether lead to satisfied customers. So, just as important as the pilot having the proper buttons, gauges and measurements in front of him/her to fly the plane under the right conditions to the desired destination, other factors come into play as well. For customers to be really satisfied with their flying experience, an aircraft has to achieve its goal, but also all other elements must be in perfect alignment: airports, traveling agencies, flight operators, flight control, passport control, luggage control, and so on. There is an entire infrastructure of processes and people working together to enable the best customer experience. Do you think they are all synchronized by chance? Did anyone think and work out how to align one process output to the next process input? All the pieces must fit together and resources must be carefully handled to serve the end result.

That's what had to happen and is still happening within the Continuous Improvement phase at Apa Nova. And that's exactly what the multiple Project

teams did. Another way of joining hands was aligning the outputs of one process to the inputs of another. Negotiating levels of Quality, Cost and Delivery
Time for all the connected processes. Creating agreement.

An example of how this works involved the HR department, and the "abuse"
of overtime hours within the operational areas. The HR department thought
that the operational teams were clocking in more hours to get extra benefits. In
contrast, the operational team found it difficult to meet its deadlines and Key
Performance Indicators with an acute shortage of personnel. Between placing
the request for a new hire until the moment that person was ready to take on
his/her daily tasks, too much time passed. The need for that extra resource was
met by doing overtime.

So, because of a lack of proper alignment between the operational processes and the recruitment process, the latter failed to perform at an acceptable rate. Unfortunately, that directly influenced the cost-related KPIs for the
operational processes – using the overtime method was much more expensive.
**This is an example of how a horizontally fragmented perception of KPIs can
directly impact the bottom line of any organization.**

The solution is a horizontal alignment of KPIs across processes and it has
the power to create the means for clearer target setting, which will be addressed
in the following sections of the book.

At the same time, a top-down approach must be taken into consideration.
Every regional or local leader of any organization that is part of a larger group
receives a set of fixed metrics that need to be measured and reported upon –
his own set of KPIs. When designing a KPI Architecture, it is important to make
sure that top-level KPIs are identified and linked to lower level KPIs. First and
foremost, the key processes that impact the measurement of top-level KPIs
have to be identified. Each process that contributes to one particular top-level
KPI must implicitly have a process KPI related to that top-level KPI.

For example, a metric related to revenue is essential in every organization.
Since revenue is usually brought in by customers, that metric is a top level KPI
to which the customer-related processes contribute the most.

At Apa Nova, revenue is mainly generated by two areas of business – the
process related to providing water and the one related to evacuating it. The KPIs
related to revenue from these two processes are consolidated into a top-level
KPI, which sums up these two revenues. That is vertical alignment.

By consolidating upwards, all relevant interactions (input – output)
within higher-level areas of responsibility were identified and compared with

each other and with lower level metrics. This was the final step in vertical and horizontal integration at all organizational levels.

Once all elements of vertical and horizontal alignment were in place, the KPI Architecture had to be strengthened by creating detailed data collection plans for each KPI, with proper operational definitions associated to measurement, analysis and performance evaluation. Without these plans, all the effort invested so far would have been in vain. As P. Drucker said: "*You can't manage what you can't measure.*"

To obtain that, several questions needed clear answers:

- Who is responsible for collecting the necessary data and where from?
- What is the frequency with which data needs to be collected?
- What are the tools that feed us relevant data at every critical control point across processes?

For accurate data collection to work as planned, people should report non-performing KPIs properly. In an organizational setup where responsibility becomes crystal clear at every level, and where the mindset is to move from an opinion-based management to a data-driven management, it is mandatory to have a bullet-proof strategy for collecting correct and accurate data. Thus, establishing a clear chain of responsibility over data collection is paramount.

Once someone is nominated for the job, he/she has to know precisely what data needs to be collected, how much and with what frequency. With the right responsibilities, the right plan and the right attitude, as well as by using a KPI Architecture that aligns KPIs and targets, both horizontally and vertically, actual data collection can begin.

Having available data enables a powerful analysis. Opening the data door into your processes helps you to make better, more informed decisions. This is process mining. It is the essence of combining the true understanding of processes and statistics, all leading to better management and data-driven decision-making.

D. From Opinion-Based Management towards Data-Driven Decisions

After the KPI Architecture had been designed, it needed to be put to good use. How do you move from having a KPI Architecture on paper to actually using it to make better and smarter decisions?

One key element never to be missed when creating such an infrastructure for data-driven decision-making, are the people enabling this system to work. You could never imagine that the pilot entering the cockpit at the beginning of a flight might lack the necessary skills to read all those metrics and use all the gauges. The amount of preparation a pilot needs before assuming the responsibility of taking a plane full of people into the air and flying it to its destination adds up to hundreds of hours of theoretical training, simulations and examinations.

Yet, in an organizational context, you can often find managers tweaking data and creating beautiful charts to support their convenient decisions. Usually, the necessary skills for that are "stolen" on the job, and there is little formal training that would ensure that the right decisions are taken. And this happens in the 21st century, way beyond the start of the digital age, in what we like to call a Knowledge Economy.

For example, any chart that plots the evolution of a process over time, without a powerful statistical engine behind it could prompt managers to take action where no action is needed or not to take action where it is needed. That translates into using unnecessary time, money and human resources to fix something that is not broken. Tampering with data is a common management mistake. Just look at how many spikes seem to need adjustment in the following Time Series Plot.

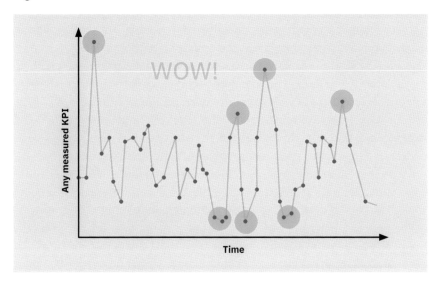

Visual representation of data (Time Series Plot example)

Imagine you were a patient in front of your doctor, and just by visually evaluating one symptom, the doctor decides you need an injection to get better. This call is based on pure intuition; there's no thermometer or thorough analysis to it.

Using statistics when looking at processes dramatically changes the quality of conversation and insight. It also opens the door to better decisions and timely controls of the processes. Any organization, and Apa Nova was no different, wants to understand the results of its processes, over time.

One tricky process that used to generate extra work at Apa Nova was "Read and establish customer water consumption". When looking at how this process behaved for certain customers, it seemed that the water-meters would once in a while provide lower readings than expected. That would usually lead to sending teams in the field to check and redo the work of reading the water-meters, only to find out that they were correct. Needless to say, this generated additional operating costs. Could they have been avoided?

The same process, when analyzed with proper graphical and statistical data-analysis tools and over a longer period of time showed a seasonal pattern of behavior from the customer. In other words, the statistical analysis supported the assumption that once in a while, people left on vacations, thus using less water. Applied to the entire population of Apa Nova customers, this single insight had the potential to cut down the re-reading by 80% and save all associated costs.

The top management team understood the potential financial benefits of using a proper statistical engine as the driving force behind data-driven decision-making for the company. They understood the need to give their employees the tools to use the KPI Architecture they created in the best possible way. A group of more than 130 employees (from key positions within all areas of the organization, like accounting, production, legal, HR, procurement, CRM and many others) had to go through a series of advanced trainings so they could understand how to use statistics in support of better business decisions.

Looking back, many people at Apa Nova agree that it was a tough challenge to handle: a no-man-left-behind strategy in Learning and Development sounds fair and honest on paper, but its implementation never comes without bottlenecks. Apa Nova was set on changing its decision-making practices in a profound way and knew that people were a key element on every level of the organization, since they were talking about a horizontal and vertical alignment of KPIs – the newly designed KPI Architecture. No room for "Garbage In – Garbage Out" type of errors.

On the flipside, getting people to change is not that simple – picture a group of 130+ individuals convincing themselves and each other that there is value in changing the decision-making process, in learning new and "complicated" tools, and having to truly believe that there is no age limit for learning. They had to be better, persevere and ultimately thrive in the new setup of the organization by applying advanced data analysis tools on a daily basis.

However, a company thrives when it is capable of having predictable outcomes. For that to happen, each process should be under control. In technical jargon, that is called having "stable processes". Statistical tools act like a magnifying glass for decision-making. Statistics can help you decide if you have stable processes, and they can show if and where to act.

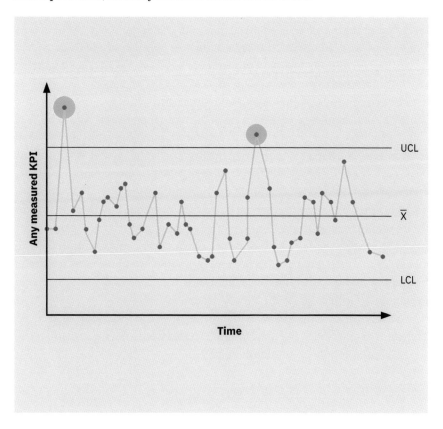

Putting statistics to work – Process Stability

Using the same process data plotted earlier and applying a powerful statistical tool (SPC) to better understand process behavior helps to determine clear upper (UCL) and lower (LCL) control limits – anything found between them represents common process behavior. This shows exactly where the abnormal process behavior is – the two red points on the graph. This drastically narrows the scope of one manager's actions for remediating the process.

After people were trained in all these advanced graphical and statistical tools, they were asked to point out how data analysis and statistics could help educate and inform better decisions when looking from above, from the seat of the CFO, or even the CEO of the organization. How can this KPI Architecture truly become a tool for them, just like the cockpit is for the pilot?

This is something that data science and statistics can help with. Once you have your processes connected through inputs and outputs, aligned both horizontally and vertically by well-crafted KPIs at both operational and management levels, process mining together with statistics can enable advanced insights that help optimize the process.

The sort of KPIs top management teams work with are more or less the same, revenue being one of them. One of the team members at Apa Nova took on the challenge to get a statistical formula for predicting revenue using actual process data. She hoped to improve her team's prediction model, which, in previous years, had failed to deliver accurate predictions by more than 15% on new and unpredictable clients. Those clients were unpredictable in their behavior and their present prediction model failed to capture that. This led to inaccurately setting budget targets. So, she and her team put their minds into creating a better statistical prediction model. She gathered representatives from all processes and started a creative process of establishing the most impactful factors that could contribute to the most accurate prediction model available. Revenue = f (factor 1, factor 2, factor 3 ... factor n)

After brainstorming and prioritizing their ideas, this team of experienced professionals concluded that the following factors were most likely to influence the response variable – Sales Prediction:

- Meter reading interval (days)
- Number of invoiced contracts
- Avg. Air Temperature (C)
- Avg. Rainfall (mc)
- Number of service-pipes

Once data was inputted into the statistical software for all of these factors, and analysis was performed, the model they had created explained more than 90% of the actual performance of sales for the selected target group. Going further and comparing that statistical model with the existing prediction model, it was statistically proven that a 72% increase in prediction accuracy would be achieved only by changing the prediction formula.

You might wonder how some of the metrics above can be controlled. They evidently do not fall under the responsibility of anyone within the organization. One example is, for certain, the real and measurable impact weather can have on water consumption patterns. But knowing exactly how much of an impact any external factor can have on your bussiness can certainly be of use. This knowledge can put you on guard and help you organize around it.

This massive effort to provide people with advanced graphical and statistical tools strengthened responsibility at all levels of the organization. It also enabled a new data-driven mindset that unlocks the potential of the new Organizational Architecture.

E. Objective Setting

Within an organizational context, objective setting is often a tense process. It's much like bargaining in a local market, negotiating who gets what budget and who delivers which results. The most vocal of merchants usually wins. Not really a picture of mature managers discussing and agreeing on targets, is it?

The main cause of all organizational problems is having a fragmented view of work, and setting objectives is no exception. That was the case of Apa Nova. As expected, the lack of accountability in regard to certain process areas created voids in responsibility. At a certain point during one of the many review meetings, this symptom became obvious and one member of the top management team immediately noted the connection between this issue and how objectives are set and achieved for the company. While reviewing the process related to repairing the water infrastructure, this particular top manager pointed out: *"I can't see which part of the processes is responsible with making sure no one steals our pipes or other bits of our infrastructure."* The person to whom this observation was addressed swiftly answered: *"We are certainly responsible with changing the pipes."* How much did it cost to entirely overlook this part of preventive activities? How should the objective of the replacement team be formulated?

Overlaps of responsibility are another symptom of the same fragmentation problem. In the phase of process identification, it was discovered that many areas of the organization were in charge of more or less the same thing. One such area was related to metering. In public services, this is a widely regulated subject. A company providing water services has strict laws and regulations regarding the level of compliance their water-meters should be at. Strict quality checks on the metering devices are done periodically, and the water-meters have to be classified as operational, so that they can be allowed within the infrastructure. The ones that fail the quality checks have to rapidly be replaced, since any reading on a non-compliant device is rendered irrelevant, under law.

Thus, it was an important objective that all the water-meters in the field were compliant – so important that it was shared by two different areas within the organization... It was confusing for them to understand this shared responsibility and this obviously implied a risk of losses.

Discussing the setting of objectives in an integrated organizational design creates a framework for correctly setting objectives at every organizational level. Every role within every process, every process within every process group, and every process group in itself has clear objectives that are linked with each other and to the company's objectives. Evaluating the performance of processes and that of the employees is directly connected with the KPI Architecture. The clear set of objectives, as well as Learning and Development can bridge the knowledge gaps of every employee who executes roles that associate with non-performing KPIs. It's all connected.

An **Integrated Organizational Design** means that all elements are developed in such a way that everything just works together. The process of building all the organizational elements in such a way is simple, but never easy. Without properly identified processes, without relevant KPIs, without an Organizational Structure to enable responsibility over the actual intended results, setting objectives can often become like setting a destination without any illustration of a map. But once all the necessary ingredients are in place, you can start a straightforward process of "Objective setting".

Since Apa Nova is part of Veolia Group – all objectives cascade from the very first organizational layer in the Group. Once they are received at company level, there needs to be a serious discussion about how to cascade them further, in the most advantageous way.

As mentioned before, the first logical organizational level would be comprised of process groups – these would become the first level in the Organizational Structure, and someone with the right skills, knowledge and abilities would receive responsibility over the process groups. Bearing that in mind, the CEO of the company has the right conversation partners under his direct management, to whom to distribute the objectives received at company level.

There are different types of objectives that can be received at company level. One found in most organizations is a critical health and safety objective: a clear objective of zero accidents is received at company level and cascades as such to the level of process group, and then further down to process levels, all the way down to role levels. Zero is zero at any level. It is up to the process owner to establish what KPIs are necessary to measure and control at his/her level of responsibility, so as to achieve that goal.

The vision for creating a safe work environment without injuries of any kind becomes an objective towards zero accidents. Therefore, this objective descends level by level, from CEO to process group owners, then further down to process owner until it reaches the lowest level of responsibility in the organization. If, historically, this was an objective associated with the Health & Safety Team KPIs, it now becomes an objective for everyone in the company.

Another generic type of objective is financially driven. How much money does the company make and at what costs? First, how much – let's say, revenue – we want to make is an objective that cascades down only to the "money making" processes. Second, all other processes within the organization cost money to execute. Any clear picture of what a customer wants should take into account what every other stakeholder requires of your organization. Targets should be set and balanced across all process groups and vertically aligned, level by level, and horizontally aligned within each level.

In this integrated view, objectives are directly linked to their corresponding KPIs – at every organizational level. They are aligned and balanced to best satisfy all the stakeholders, in the order of their importance to the company. The KPI Architecture is thus complete.

The company now looks at success in a very different way. The vertically and horizontally integrated KPI infrastructure allows for everyone at every level – from the smallest role all the way to high-level multi-process employees – to quantify their contribution to the overall success of the company. This was achieved while preserving all critical stakeholder KPIs, and is backed by a 35% overall decrease in the number of management KPIs across all levels.

Performance management also moved from opinion-based to advanced graphical and statistical analysis, using advanced statistical software and insight-driven decision-making. This made room for a culture in which data is not used to control people, but instead to give them a new layer of knowledge to understand and improve their work.

6. Risk Management: Preparing for the Worst when Everything Is Going Great

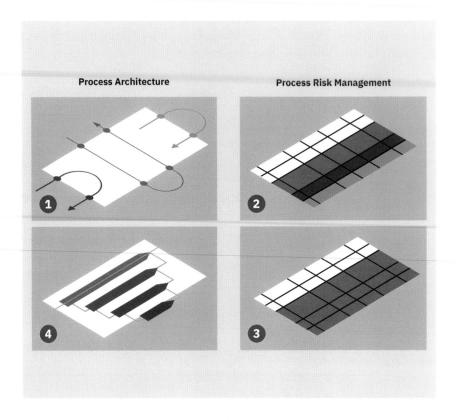

Prevention has often been associated with wisdom. Preventing bad things from happening got us to this point in history, when almost anything we envision is possible. Even so, humanity wasn't always blessed with the wisest rulers and leaders. Wisdom implies judgement, and judgement is a **process**.

We can look at prevention as a result of a process, can't we? How should we begin such a process? It's fair to presume that we **only** want to prevent undesired events from happening. Thus, the first logical step is to identify those events that could happen in the future and could negatively impact us and our objectives. Whether we call them undesired events, threats, liabilities, or potential hazards, it's all about the concept of **risk**.

Is it enough to just expect for the best in the future? Or would it be more useful to know the prioritized risks, based on a real evaluation? If you were a real gambler, you'd probably bet on the second option. This entire process is about identifying, analyzing and mitigating risks, and is generally known as Risk Management. This chapter describes the challenges of implementing Failure Mode and Effects Analysis (FMEA) – one of the best Risk Management methodologies in the world – at Apa Nova.

A. Advanced Risk Management

The implementation of this Risk Management methodology began in March, 2017. All the steps that had been taken until that point (described in the previous sections) had created the mindset and knowledge needed by both management and employees to successfully implement Failure Mode and Effects Analysis. A strong knowledge about data-driven decision-making, KPIs, and process-driven Organizational Structure boosted the enthusiasm about embracing a risk-based approach of all activities, as Risk Management was a "territory still under exploration" for the company at that moment.

Before March, 2017, there were several different forms of risk assessment, specific to a small number of departments. Simply put, a risk-based approach means that the company should be aware of and prepared for all the risks it might be exposed to. Why is it really so important for any company *to prepare for the worst when everything seems to perform well?* Why is Risk Management so important after all? Most of us agree that the better you prepare, the better you plan, the greater your chances of achieving your objectives.

Imagine you are planning a well-deserved vacation. This is a process we've all been through many times, and possibly the one you prepare for the most and with the most joy! For many of us, this preparation is probably based on a very thorough risk assessment, and we might not even be aware that we are doing it. Let's say you decide for next year's summer vacation to go camper vanning in Iceland for two weeks. This is the starting point of your planning process. Now, the hard and fun part begins:

- When is the best time to go on that trip, according to the weather forecast?
- When can both you and your better half plan your summer leave?
- How many weeks ahead should you buy airline tickets in order to get a fair price?
- Where can you find the campervan that suits your needs, available for rental at that time of year?

- Are there campsites on your planned itinerary, and are there camping spots available in that period?
- How do you decide your itinerary under these conditions?

And the list goes on. When all the answers are ready, you have a plan with clear objectives. So, naturally, most of your decisions involve performing a risk assessment.

The main goal is to experience one of the best times of your life, which means achieving all the goals mentioned above, right? You start thinking about what might go wrong that could interfere with your plans:

- What are the chances of it being cold that time of year?
- What can happen at work, and what is the probability for those things to happen, thus getting in the way of your vacation?
- What can go wrong for you to miss the flight?

And so on.

The next step, probably, is to think more deeply about those problems that seem serious at first, judging by the probability of occurrence and the effect that they could have on your holiday objectives. Of course, you should add in the mix your personal "risk appetite".

The concept of "risk appetite"[2] helps guide the actions of an organization and its approach to risk and Risk Management. These actions include all the necessary steps you must go through preemptively, prior to your holiday, and all the possible solutions in case something does go wrong.

For instance, some things can't be prevented (like weather), but you can be prepared by packing the right gear. Other things do not require thorough planning, as their impact is minimal. For these things, it is enough to take some extra cash or clothing. But some things are crucial for your vacation, like not missing your flight. For this, many of us use checklists of required documents, reminders of when to leave, traffic information, etc. These are just basic tools that help mitigate risks.

After this short exercise you probably came to realize how many events can interfere with your daily life objectives, and how you unconsciously take

---

2   According to ISO 31000, which is the standard for Risk Management, risk appetite is the "amount and type of risk that an organization is prepared to pursue, retain or take".

preventive actions, basically performing daily risk assessments and contin-
gency planning. Amazing, right?

Let's move on. Think about how a company should address risks and why a risk-based approach should be in its DNA. A company doesn't have its own judgement, its actions are the expression of a "collective mind", aligned and synchronized through corporate governance. Its reason to exist is to meet its stakeholders' expectations. Think of how many objectives are set in a company, and how all of them are part of its complex strategy.

Imagine how many events can occur and how they can correlate in order to alter the fulfilment of those objectives. But how about the risks? How many companies are interested in managing their risks? How can a "collective mind" evaluate and prioritize risk for a company to function better?

The implementation of FMEA methodology for each and every process faced Apa Nova with some challenges. Once the methodology is well understood, the FMEA process itself seems straightforward, but is it really that simple? Is there a "one size fits all" Risk Management methodology that can be applied to every single company in the world? Wouldn't that be nice?

Each company must tailor fit the assessment tools used in the FMEA process to its own needs. In fact, this is the key to success. A tailored fit Risk Management methodology means that the way you look at risk is finely tuned to the company's risk appetite, which in fact should be strongly related to business strategy. This makes all the difference in how well a company addresses the needs of its stakeholders.

Why one method and what does it mean? This question had no answer in Apa Nova before March, 2017. Everybody knew that risks are assessed and managed by "one department in the company" and that was enough. Indeed, many risks were properly managed, especially those related to Operations, and Health and Safety. Managing these risks is paramount for Veolia and Apa Nova, as Responsibility is one of their core values. But what about other risks?

Each department that had a risk-based approach embedded in its activities performed the risk assessment analysis in its own way. And that meant that nothing was standardized or measurable across the company. Of course, that also implies no cross-company centralized Risk Management dashboard that could be used by management.

With such a Risk Management philosophy, an issue emerged: some stakeholder needs weren't considered. An honest answer to all these problems is the implementation of one single Risk Management methodology in the entire company.

B. A Common Framework for Your Risk Appetite

There are multiple angles from which to approach a Risk Management analysis.

First, there is System FMEA or SFMEA, which helps to keep the focus on an entire system made out of many and complex processes, like an oil rig in the North Sea. SFMEA ensures that the entire infrastructure produces its output the way it was intended to in the Design Phase, keeping track of all its identified potential failure modes.

Then comes Design FMEA or DFMEA, which is concerned with thinking out and assessing the Design of a Product prior to physically making it. DFMEA will support the Design Phase and it will identify potential undesired functional elements of the product and their related effects and causes.

This is then followed by Process Failure Mode and Effects Analysis or PFMEA, and at this phase in the Project, this was the optimal starting point. As the name suggests it, PFMEA is designed and used **to identify risks for each process step as early as possible.**

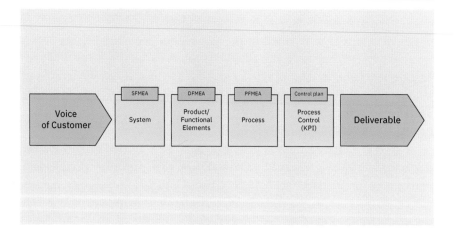

The first activity of a PFMEA methodology process is identifying the functions of a process (process steps). Next, potential failure modes are identified for each identified function or process step. This refers to scenarios in which the observed function could potentially fail, thus the entire Project could fail as a result. For each potential failure mode there are several potential effects on the overall process. So, up until this point, PFMEA methodology was used to identify the potential failure modes and their potential effects.

When discussing the potential failure mode of processes, blinded by the desire of meeting the process requirements, many people had a hard time accepting that it was possible for undesirable things to happen: *"What do you mean by not delivering water to our clients? It can't happen, it's impossible!"*; *"What do you mean by not generating the invoice? This is why we are here!"*

Over time, they discovered the real meaning of the likelihood of occurrence, as well as the meaning of the concept of probable events – what was realistically possible to happen even if the experience they had had until that point had not confirmed it.

The next step is to quantify these effects by determining the severity of their impact, identify potential causes of failure and determine their probability of occurrence, as well as assess the implemented methods to prevent potential causes or detect causes or effects. In order to adapt the FMEA methodology to Apa Nova's specific needs, an internal cross-functional team was appointed and given the objective of tailoring the FMEA methodology. This would help create customized scales for Severity, Occurrence, Detection assessment and a Classification matrix, based on all relevant stakeholders.

This team, comprised of members of the Integrated Management System and Internal Audit, worked closely with Advanced Thinking, in order to draft specific instruments that would best suit the company's needs. These tools were validated by many other areas of expertise within the company, such as Finance, Environment, Production area, Distribution and Supply Chain.

When we refer to a process, we equally refer to its stakeholders. As mentioned before, a process cannot exist without the stakeholder's requirement and expectation of a deliverable. Consequently, when we assess the Severity, the impact an effect has on a process and its output, we have its stakeholder's request in mind. This was vital for adapting the severity assessment scale to the needs of the company.

In case an effect of the failure mode appears, it is very likely that one or more KPIs will not be met, thus we will then have to deal with Non-Performing KPIs and the Cost of Poor Quality. For example, a potential failure mode of the "Hire new personnel" process was the failure to supply the requested human resource to the "Provide water" process.

Providing water can't stop because an operator is missing. The only solution is to increase the overtime hours of the existing operators so that targets can be met. This would generate additional costs for the "Provide water" process, much higher than getting a new hire on board. This shows how all these elements fit together and rely on each other because they are all meant to be integrated.

The main objective of implementing a single Risk Management methodology in the entire company was for it to be applicable to all processes and at all levels of decision. This meant that PFMEA Risk Management should be every process owner's responsibility and should be consolidated at company level.

This type of assessment should be performed by the people who know the process best. If the Severity Assessment Scale was expressed only from the perspective of the financial impact, it could have become difficult to use and it would have been incomplete for many processes. The process teams could not have easily quantified the amount of money spent, or even lost.

If a manager needed to take mitigation actions on several different risks, how could he decide which situation was more critical? Imagine having three potential risks in front of you: the potential risk for human accidents because of not properly securing the work perimeter, the potential financial risk of not complying to GDPR regulations, and the potential environmental risk of dumping untreated wastewater into a large river.

Which one is the worst? How would you decide which one to address, given the reality of limited resources? Imagine all managers in the company facing the same decision. Without an integrated framework, there is no way to compare risks.

To solve that, the cross-functional team performed an inventory of all relevant stakeholders of the company and drafted a multi-criteria severity assessment scale comprised of 6 different perspectives, to assess the impact an effect of a potential failure mode can have on any type of stakeholder. They decided to combine relevant perspectives in order to obtain an accurate Severity scale, making all types of risks comparable in terms of Severity. Those perspectives referred to stakeholder safety, operation continuity, financial loss, reputation, legal liability, and the communication and relationship with regulatory bodies.

For each of those perspectives, a 10-level assessment scale was designed, where level 1 represents a minimal impact and level 10 a maximal impact of an identified effect. There were 6 individual assessment scales embedded into a single Severity assessment tool. They had to use as many perspectives as they needed, according to the data available to them at that time.

The main benefit of using a multi criteria assessment instrument like this one is that it challenges users to switch perspectives and evaluate more than one side of an effect, obviously those for which data is available. The final score is the one that rates highest on any of the 6 perspectives.

Moreover, using this assessment tool meant that, from the highest perspective of the company, a risk from HR impact area, for example, could be

quantified in the same way as an operational risk. This created the opportunity for risk prioritization across all processes, a major shift in thinking in
the company.

The next challenge for the team was to adapt the Occurrence Assessment
Scale to the company's specific needs. Occurrence refers to the probability of
a cause to materialize. This materialization of the causes of failure modes represents the probability that these will occur as the process is executed.

This time, the challenge was to quantify the frequency of all types of processes (for example, the "Report financial status" process that is executed a
few times a year as opposed to the "Answer customer claims" process, executed several times every day), because frequency may vary from one specific
company to another. Hence, designing a single assessment scale that could be
applied regardless of this diversity of process frequency was highly necessary.

The impact of occurrence in risk level evaluation is significant, as the
higher the probability of a cause to appear, the higher the risk. It's one thing
that, for 100 runs of the "Provide invoice" process, there is a probability of 1%
for the occurrence of a cause that leads to incorrect invoices; it's a completely
different thing to find that there is a probability of 15% for the occurrence of that
cause. The risk level in the second case is obviously higher than in the first case.

The third assessment scale (after Severity and Occurrence) is Detection –
being aware of the probability of cause occurrence. The FMEA methodology
requires a Detection rating for each identified cause or failure mode. Here, the
challenge was to accept that true detection is done by the organization before
the customer notices it, otherwise it becomes redundant and can no longer be
considered detection.

For example, online analyzers are installed at the Production of Drinking
Water Plant, to send an immediate alarm to the dispatcher's dashboard if some
measurable values regarding the quality characteristics of the water are above
or below the accepted values. Therefore, the dispatcher will be able to take the
necessary preventive measures, so that the final output will not be affected in
any way.

In contrast, the Detection of the cause can only be made after the effect has
occurred and no prevention measures can be taken. The degree of Detection
may vary from a higher level, when automated detection of the causes is in
place, to using human inspection, or to causes that cannot even be detected.

As the meetings progressed and people started to work with this methodology, it became clear that having no prior experience meant people
would not properly understand and apply the scales right away. For instance,

understanding a 5 rating on the Occurrence scale means a 50% possibility of a failure mode cause to appear. The Advanced Thinking team had to help the Project teams along to find the best values, based on their experience.

One other revelation was the importance of correctly assessing Severity, Occurrence and Detection; the teams would later understand that it's harder to address some ratings as opposed to others: the detection rating of a failure mode can easily be influenced by improving the detection method, while the severity of the failure mode never changes unless you change the process itself.

After determining all this, the classical approach of FMEA is to assess the failure modes according to the Risk Priority Number (RPN), the multiplication between Severity, Occurrence and Detection. But is it fair? Let's look at the next example:

Activity/ Function	Failure Mode	Severity	Occurrence	Detection	RPN
1	A	9	1	5	45
2	B	1	5	9	45
3	C	5	9	1	45

Three different failure modes with the same RPN

The Risk Priority Number is the same for all three failure modes, but do you consider them all equally important?

In order to resolve this issue and to adapt the methodology even further to the company's requirements, the top management team agreed to introduce additional criteria to facilitate a proper prioritization of risks and their Risk Priority Number: Risk Classification. This takes into consideration Severity and Occurrence, their combination being crucial in risk evaluation.

Classification determines which failure mode is too risky and needs to be addressed first, depending on the company's overall "positioning regarding risks", or, if you can recall our jolly vacation planning, the *risk appetite*.

The Classification Assessment Scale consists of a matrix combining Severity and Occurrence, both graded on a scale from 1 to 10. Based on a graphical representation, risks are classified, from "acceptable risks" all the way to "critical risks".

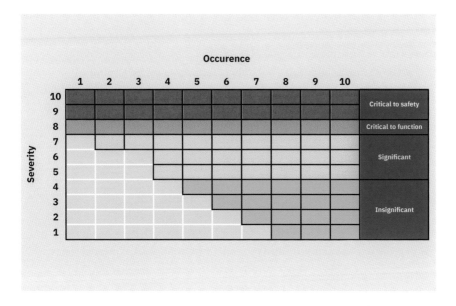

Classification Assessment Scale

Based on these principles, the Project teams at Apa Nova had to decide what represents Critical to Safety, Significant, Nonsignificant or even Accepted risk. This framework must be adapted to the realities of any company. Also, the Project teams created examples of applied methodology using Apa Nova's processes from 3 different areas: Purchasing, Environment and Financial. Only after all failure modes are classified, the priority of mitigation actions is determined using RPN to differentiate within each class.

After management's approval and validation of the assessment scales, a series of FMEA workshops were conducted with employees from all departments. These workshops provided the best environment for implementing the methodology throughout the company, as well as brainstorming sessions to evaluate the assessment scales provided.

In line with the down-to-earth approach of the Project, the management team decided to implement Risk Management in phases. The first phase was managing risks at process level. A more detailed view of Risk Management, for the activities within each process, was to be tackled in the Continuous Improvement phase of the Project.

Top management decided that during the FMEA meetings, the Risk Analysis had to be performed by the same employees who mapped the processes that were already underway.

After all these steps, the designated team standardized a single Procedure of Risk Management to be rigorously implemented in all departments of Apa Nova.

During a Risk Management meeting, one of the middle managers, who had previously been very skeptical about the Project, approached one of the partners from Advanced Thinking and whispered: *"If we will use this Risk Management process, then all our risk-related problems that get our production process bogged down from time to time will be solved."*

The Failure Modes and Effects Analysis methodology implementation was achieved for all processes and meant an alignment of Risk Management practices across the company. It slowly created a risk culture, a coherent risk vocabulary and knowledge base across all departments of Apa Nova.

As a result, more than 20% of the risks were reclassified, some becoming strategic to the company and others proving to be overinflated concerns coming from a fragmented perspective. Several high-level risk reduction projects were undertaken within the company. Most importantly, a lively conversation now exists around the severity of risks, the controllable parts of risks, disaster response and other key aspects related to the topic.

Moving further, the implementation of the methodology will begin at role level within the entire company, allowing risks to be managed in a truly integrated way.

7. Learning for Performance: The Process Role-Driven Competency Map

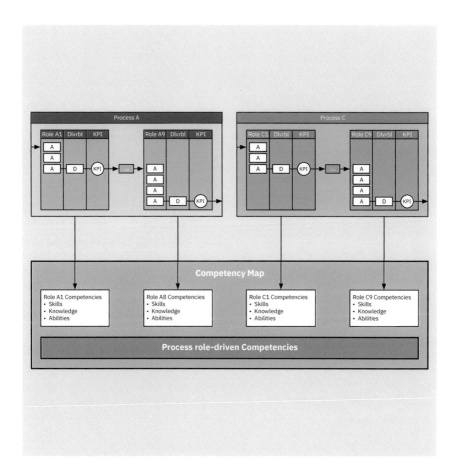

Redesigning Apa Nova's processes clarified the difference between performing an activity and achieving an end result that would be valuable to the stakeholders. It became self-evident that none of the activities, taken individually, created anything of value for the stakeholders. Only when they were all put together in the right order was value achieved.

People became aware that they were playing different roles in different processes. The process redesign led to new, more complex roles which placed new demands on the people who executed them. The work of these employees changed, as well as what was required of them. It was not just about performing an activity and looking for the boss' approval or seeking ways to please him. First and foremost, it was about taking responsibility for the results. Once people were empowered to take full responsibility, this implied management and leadership skills, as well as the authority to make important decisions.

The most interesting responsibility in this context is the responsibility related to the process roles. This was crucial to the correct configuration of Apa Nova's competency map.

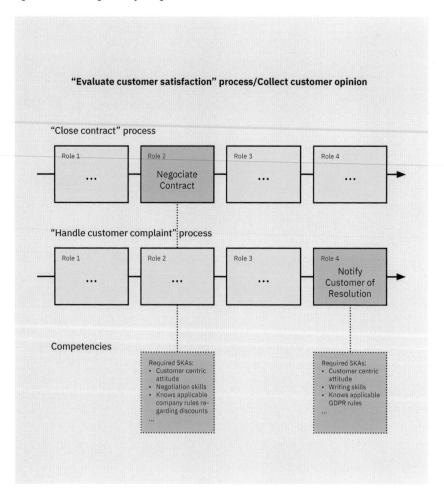

An example of process role-driven competencies map

In contrast to the traditional view, where competencies pop up from job descrip- tions that often hide grey areas and overlaps, process role-driven competencies are a result of summing up all the skills, knowledge and abilities that are required by each role played by any individual.

All process role-driven competencies are specific, because they represent those skills, knowledge and abilities that are needed to perform all the required activities at a certain standard. Mapping the processes at these levels – role and activity – brings to attention that some of these specific competencies may be common, hence could be standardized at company level. We refer to them as generic competencies. For example, one's ability to self-manage is fundamental and vital to anyone performing any activity within any role in the Process Architecture. The intensity of using this ability differs.

Slowly, the specific and generic process role-driven competencies became the two main components of Apa Nova's new competency map. It was not the concept, but the perspective behind the concept that challenged people.

In the traditional way of work, the individual contribution to the result was almost impossible to determine. In contrast, after the shift in thinking, which the Reengineering Project facilitated, the responsibility for process end results *"offered a cold and indisputable gauge of performance"* (M. Hammer). This could be directly linked to each process role and its performance. Another way to say this is that individual work was going to be evaluated in relation to process performance. Like a double-edged blade, it motivated some and discouraged others.

People play a central role in the success of any organization. They can achieve superior performance only by constantly accumulating knowledge, seeking new ways to approach issues and an attitude characterized by motivation and discipline. Such a mindset can be a gold-mine for those who truly understand it. They will learn to think and act according to it.

In this new framework, competencies are directly linked to process roles and process roles have a measurable contribution to process performance. Poor process role performance can be addressed by targeting those competencies that need improving. Thus, targeted Learning and Development Programs can be designed.

From a psychological standpoint, the implications of the paradigm shift brought about by the Reengineering Project were intense. They went far beyond any existent practices at that moment in managing human resources at Apa Nova. Expressed or not, this new perspective raised many questions in the minds and hearts of people. Sometimes, you just had to look into people's eyes to figure out what they were thinking. You could see them worrying whether they were going to succeed in the new roles they designed. At the same time, you could read excitement in their eyes, similar to an entrepreneur's who finally has the freedom to shape his/her future, being responsible for any failure or success, and constantly integrating and relevant knowledge.

This is called learning for performance. In other words, a dedication of doing daily work not for show, nor just for the sake of performance evaluations, but because the roles one performs in a company are meaningful to the person.

8. Crystal Clear Job Descriptions

From Process Identification to Individual Responsibility

Altogether, the Process Architecture, the KPI Architecture and the Organizational Structure enabled Apa Nova to start rethinking the way their Job Descriptions presented the job that each employee had to do.

The new Job Descriptions would be made by carefully extracting and assigning all the relevant roles to every employee. Generally, this is the job of the process owner, in collaboration with all the heads of the departments through which the processes pass. Basically, the Job Descriptions would become the document in which every employee would find the sum of his/her process roles within the company. The content of this document was already created in the process maps. Every process role, activity, deliverable and KPI would have to be transferred in a document to show what each person in Apa Nova does.

This way, the Job Description of an electrician working in the Production department would become the collection of all the process roles that person was assigned to within all the processes: "Perform installation maneuvers", "Treat major Pumping Station malfunctions", "Maintain installations" and so on until all the process roles he has to perform have been extracted from the actual process maps.

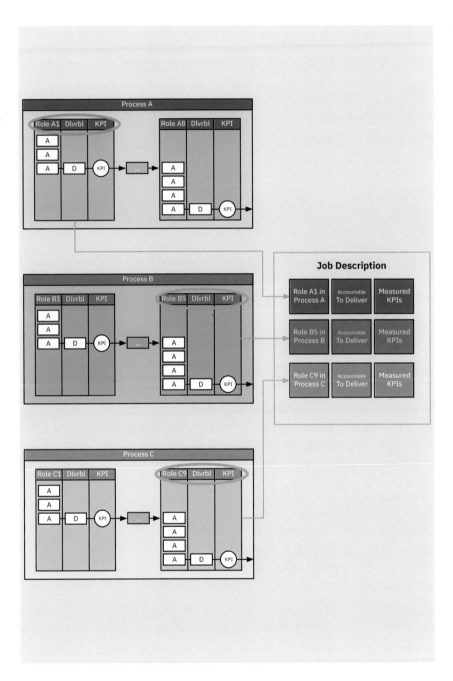

Process-driven Job Descriptions

Understanding how work was done, really identifying all processes and creating the Process Architecture in the organization was the foundation for everything that followed. It opened the path to properly defining individual responsibility.

Because so many people were involved in the Project from the very beginning from every level of the company – thus becoming the architects of their future organization – it wasn't difficult at all for them to accept and adopt the newly developed Job Descriptions.

The Job Description became the personalized map of every employee – it showed everyone what they had to do in each process (their roles), what was expected of them to deliver (their deliverables), and how their work would be measured (their KPIs). This level of clarity, visibility and connection to the actual processes had never been previously achieved at Apa Nova.

One more ingredient was missing to turn this piece of the puzzle into a success story in its own right: the automatic extraction of Job Descriptions, directly from the process maps. Developing an in-house software application to do just that became an objective and soon after, a reality.

In a review meeting, after seeing how difficult it was for people to agree upon and document what they do within the company, a member of the top management team remarked:

> *"We can agree that if you carefully observe professionals doing their job, you can 'steal' their knowledge of the craft. Now I understand why this is so true – it's 'stolen' because it isn't documented anywhere. My ardent wish is for us to create an environment for Learning."*

The roles people had redesigned were now becoming their written, agreed upon, day-to-day responsibility. They would also be directly linked to the actual deliverables of their job and to the KPIs that would become the foundation of a data-driven Employee Performance and Learning Management System.

Process role-based Job Descriptions mean that what you have in your Job Description is what the organization expects you to do. As one manager put it:

> *"the Job Description is a description of what you do in the company's interest, nothing more, nothing less."*

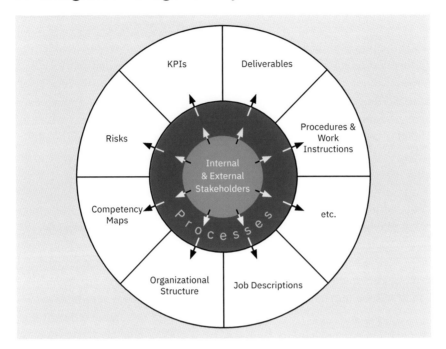

It is common practice in organizations that this is a task for the Quality Team, the ones responsible with all the Standards and the Management System – "the librarians" of the organization. They jot down what you do into a neat document, which is then indexed and shelved for safe-keeping, just like a book waiting for someone to come and read it.

In the beginning of the Project, Apa Nova's process documentation existed and was seemingly well-kept. But when asked how much of the procedures were applied in real life, people mostly shrugged their shoulders or dropped their gaze. Furthermore, when asked if they were ever involved in creating the required process documents, people started smiling. This is one main change achieved through the Reengineering Project!

Historically, as it has been already pointed out, process maps, KPI-related documents, risk registries, procedures and work instructions were created by people at different moments in time, for different reasons and from fragmented perspectives; all the knowledge the company possessed was scattered around different departments, chaperoned by different people with different interests. In the Project framework for creating an integrated Process Architecture with every organizational element carefully designed and integrated into the other, it was time to completely redesign how knowledge was documented and preserved within Apa Nova.

In its purest form, a Management System should be the core documenting system of the organization – the place with all the best knowledge from everyone contributing to the company – a place to gather and keep all the Strategies, Business Rules, Procedures, the Processes and everything else that documents how the company works. It is a living organism that grows with the company and its people. **When well implemented, a Management System has the capacity to revert the well known fact that 80% of how an organization truly operates lies only in the heads of its employees.**

By this point, you've probably realized that, by redesigning Apa Nova's organizational elements, the Project teams had worked together to develop comprehensive documentation of how the company works, the content of the future Management System. But up until then, all these documents (process maps, risk registry, KPIs and operational definition, etc.) had been kept among Project documents. For them to become official documentation, they had to be transferred into the new Integrated Management System of the company.

The same people who built all the elements of the organization had to create their Management System, the framework to hold all that content. A cross-functional team was assembled, which was meant to create a system that responded to everyone's needs, much more than an old library to be forgotten, a living library for all to use. The guiding principle behind this was to avoid redundancies and rework.

The first step in redesigning the Management System was to collect all the existing types of documents. They were then analyzed to understand all the information they contained. Finally, the team had to decide which information had to be kept and in what type of document within the new Documentation Architecture.

Processes are the backbone of the entire documentation system, because all the other organizational elements connect back to the information contained in the process maps. Building upon this, and the necessity to keep the new system organized as times goes by, the team decided to create a custom coding logic, through which all the elements would be linked together.

A most welcomed effect of keeping it all together and integrated was the reduction of endless internal audits from different and fragmented perspectives: no more process audits, internal control audits, management system audits, conformity audits, etc. Instead, there would be one integrated audit, from all possible angles, which saved everyone a lot of time.

Going beyond documentation, Apa Nova's Integrated Management System has become a knowledge platform containing the critical elements that describe and interconnect the company. While fully compliant with all current Quality Management System Standards, it is also the foundation for the future Continuous Improvement efforts of the company, ready to grow in future developments.

Food for thought:

- Who are all your stakeholders and what do they expect from you?
- What are the processes that work to meet those expectations?
- How do you evaluate the performance of your processes?
- How should you manage your processes to ensure responsibility over the demands of each of your stakeholders?
- How can your processes fail to deliver and how can you prepare to mitigate that risk?
- How should you develop people's competencies to maximize process performance?
- How do you link what needs to be done with what every individual is responsible with?
- How do you capture and maintain the knowledge of your organization?

CHAPTER 3

The Journey to the First Place in the World

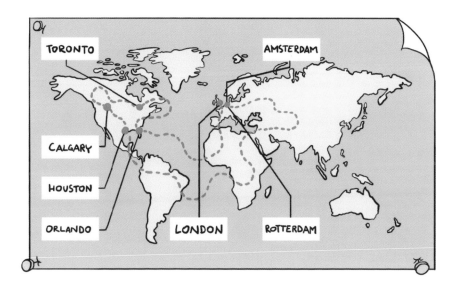

In the beginning of the Project, the top management team of Apa Nova and the Advanced Thinking team had a serious discussion about the future, which resulted in the creation of the Master Plan. One of the questions at that point was: "how do we evaluate the success of a Project of this magnitude and scope?" The answer was two-fold:

First of all, Apa Nova's results as a company would have to speak for themselves in a measurable and relevant way, as you are going to see below.

Secondly, the design of the Project would have to stand up against the highest international standards in the field. This meant competing on the European and then global stage within the Business Improvement Community, to gain proper external validation for the entire Project.

Moreover, if the structured approach to bring the company back on track would prove successful, all of the parties agreed that the methodology would be a valuable knowledge base that was worth sharing. The plan was set-up so that, after one year, the Project would become a public contender, first on the European stage, and then aiming for the First Place in the World – the race was on!

1. Exceeding All Stakeholder Expectations

Imagine Apa Nova, a company that, at the beginning of the Project, was under the burden of overcomplicated processes, traditional management thinking and weak leadership. How far could it go within a three years timespan?

As with any other project, there comes a time to do the math. Hence, this section presents some of the critical gains of Apa Nova after the Reengineering Project, as well as the key qualitative differences. It answers to that particular question that you might have in mind: was the whole effort worth it for Apa

Nova? Just as in the beginning of the Project, the key gains and improvements of the company will be seen from the perspectives of its stakeholders: Customers, Authorities, the City of Bucharest, Shareholders, and Employees.

A. Faster and Better for the Customer

From a company operating in an industry that usually thinks of its customers as "captive", Apa Nova slowly shifted into a customer-oriented organization, while also keeping an eye on the business benefits.

KPIs regarding the responsiveness of customer-oriented processes improved dramatically. For example:

- The necessary time to diagnose a fault, which improved by 96% in comparison to earlier practices;
- The necessary time to repair water faults, which registered an 86% drop in duration for that type of intervention;
- The average response time to any formal request made by any stakeholder decreased by 88%;
- The voice of the customers became increasingly important and it sharpened the company's focus even more. As a consequence, new front offices were built for better customer experience;
- The company's customers were warmly impressed. The number of complaints dropped by 24%.

The changes got public attention and, slowly, Apa Nova's reputation improved among customers and other stakeholders.

B. Civic Engagement

In addition to maximizing the value of stakeholders, Apa Nova gave a sense of pride to the citizens of Bucharest by partnering with the Municipality to reconstruct the city's historic fountain chain (www.apanovabucuresti.ro/simfonia-apei). This endeavor had such an amplitude that it won the World Record Academy award for the "Longest Choreographed Fountain System". Due to the nature of their business, this was an act of corporate social responsibility that the company chose to do for the benefit of the local community.

The new mindset also induced the leverages for better communication strategies and especially helped resolve delays in the communication with local authorities. For example, the new, significantly higher speed of Apa Nova's First

Responder Teams enabled them to arrive to faults in the public domain faster than any other public infrastructure operator and, if needed, to secure the area for pedestrians and coordinate with the proper operator. It reflects the dedication of Apa Nova to adopt the role of a change agent, thus creating a sense of urgency to improve collaboration among actors in the local market, to serve the citizens of Bucharest.

C. Stabilizing, Growing and Expanding: Shareholder Perspective

In the beginning of the Reengineering Project, Apa Nova was facing difficulties in achieving some operational targets. Every new objective, such as cost reduction, was seen as a chore, creating endless quarrels about how the new targets would be achieved. Within the first two years of the Project, the situation had been totally turned around in the minds of shareholders:

- The overall improvements of all the reengineered processes generated hard benefits representing almost 8% of yearly sales for the following two years;
- In addition, freed-up operational capability generated a 49% increase of added sales from other services (mostly network installation and maintenance contracts);
- The new figures allowed Apa Nova to gain a new stance in front of the Veolia Group, generating enough trust to start implementing a company acquisition Project that increased Veolia's presence in Romania from 5 to 8 companies, also marking the Group's only core-business (public water utilities) acquisition in 2018.

Overall, the company had a new badge of trust from all its shareholders, private and public, and was on a new path of development and growth.

D. A Better Employer

The relationship with its employees had long been a pain point within Apa Nova. The relationship between management and the employee's Union had reached a critical point. But massively involving the company's employees in the Business Transformation Project also turned this around, opening lines of communication and collaboration that had previously been closed. All the effort people put into rebuilding the company from the ground up was also literally rewarding:

- The average net wage went up by 10%;
- Employees, who are shareholders in Apa Nova, also received significant dividends in the two years following the start of the Project;
- The overall lower labor costs decreased by 6%, and labor productivity went up by 49%;
- Resources were invested in the development of a new Vocational Education and Training Project, to educate and attract young talents into the field – offering massive practical experience and significant scholarships – with optional employment opportunities for graduates;
- With the employee in mind, a new fleet of operational vehicles were purchased, increasing the capability and safety of field activities;
- Existing facilities were upgraded to higher standards of safety and comfort, and new ones were contracted for better work conditions.

Making the company's turnaround a project for its employees deeply changed the culture of the organization, enabling people to reshape their future in a very tangible way.

These direct results were produced by the changes in the organizational elements of the company. This redesigned skeleton was the key that opened the critical structural locks in the company and created room for more change to happen. It generated that shift in thinking that finally led to a total shift in practice.

These figures and achievements – it is obvious even from the outside – are not just an accountant's pen strokes or the classical results of downsizing. They come from an integrated approach to company transformation that gives a sense of how the company has dramatically improved as a system.

Altogether, these results and figures simply exceeded the shareholders' expectations. They also showed that it's easy to look good on the outside if you truly have a healthy body. In consequence, they encouraged Apa Nova to take continuous actions towards progress and to step onto the World Stage of Business Transformation.

2. Taking Off on the International Level

The first contact of the Project with an international audience happened in April 2017 at the OPEX Week – Business Transformation Europe Summit in London. Members of the Project management team went there to meet their European counterparts and find out what the current leaders involved in similar projects from all over the continent thought about Business Transformation. They felt it was only natural to make sure that what Apa Nova was doing was not just an isolated project in a country of the CEE region, but that it could compete at European level and become a valuable case study for the community.

From presentations, panel debates and informal discussions they understood that what Apa Nova was facing in their current business reality was similar, in principle, to everyone else. They had the same strategic concerns, problems in managing change, structural obstacles and dilemmas in their respective organizational cultures.

Having assessed the conversation around Business Transformation on the European stage, the next step was to move on to international experts. People in Apa Nova realized that their efforts were in line with the most advanced theories and practice in the field, and also that the progress of the Project at that point, after more than one year of hard work, was just the beginning. The road to a fundamental Bussiness Transformation is never-ending, and it requires a sturdy mindset of continuous learning, as well as a strong willingness to improve.

After these interactions, the Project management team felt they were ready to start showing the world what Apa Nova was working on. The first public presentation of the Project happened at the HR Vision Event in Amsterdam, in 2017. It addressed the fundamental People Component built into the Master Plan, both from a structural perspective (how the key of the future Apa Nova was to be the true fit between people's jobs and the way they are selected and trained) and from a change of management perspective. It was well received and the Project management team facilitated a lot of productive conversations during the presentation and during workshops.

More importantly, the way people received the presentation gave every-body the courage to go on.

3. Achieving European Recognition

Within the first year, the Project gained more exposure than expected. Only one week after HR Vision, the Project management team was invited to present at the PEX Europe event in Amsterdam. It was a chance to demonstrate the entire Project logic and address questions from the audience. The title of the presentation was "Drive change, improvement and innovation for both your internal and external customers" and it created a huge buzz. The Q&A Session went beyond anything the team could have hoped – dozens of questions flowed from the audience, especially about the integration of organizational elements.

The answers generated even more questions from the public, so many that the session went beyond the allotted time and organizers had to insist on the team leaving the stage. To their surprise, several people from the audience left the conference room to talk to the team off-stage, insisting on knowing more. At this point, it became clear that the Project was undoubtedly relevant to a wide audience. It was not only methodologically sound and practically relevant, but it also gave answers to questions people avoided asking.

As these events were unfolding, the European Business Process Excellence community was paying attention and wanted to find out more. This popularity curve culminated with an invitation to submit a full report of the Project in that year's annual publication. The report itself was highly appreciated and made the cut as one of the 4 contributors in the "Major Transformation in European Companies that are reshaping the business Landscape" PEX Europe Publication 2017.

4. Knocking on the Door of a Worldwide Audience

That same year, the Project was showcased within the Global State of Process Excellence Annual Report – Empowering Business Growth. Soon after, the Project management team decided to see what the Global Stage of Organizational Transformation looked like. They headed out to the 19th Annual OPEX Week Business Transformation World Summit 2018, in Florida.

The presentation took place during one of the plenary Keynote Panels, under the title "A Large Scale, Complete Turn-around Transformation Case Study: How Veolia Drives Significant Efficiency and Growth from their Courageous Business Process and Architecture Reengineering Project".

Once again, the room became lively and the questions ran overtime. At the end of the day, the organizers encouraged the Project management team to submit the Project as part of the PEX Awards for the Best Business Transformation Project. The team left feeling inspired, and also with a few other invitations to present the Project and its accomplishments. Three more international conferences followed in 2018: "Optimizing Safety, Efficiency, Sustainability and

"Drive Business Transformation through Modern Methods of Process Excellence" PEX Rotterdam 2018 and "Operational Excellence in Energy & Utilities" OPEX Toronto 2018.

All the positive feedback, the interest shown by the international audience, and, especially, the already promising results of the on-going implementation (only 3 years into the Project), encouraged the Project management team to submit the Project in the competition for the Best Business Transformation Project in the World.

5. Reaching the First Place in the World

From the very beginning, the goal of competing on the international level was to come out on top, so as to gain external confirmation that the Project was a best-practice example in the field. Competing for the Best Business Transformation Project meant two things:

First, unraveling all the methodological aspects that had contributed to each key decision within the Project. In spite of all the foreseeable deviations of a real-life implementation of such a large-scale and full-scope Project, there was clear method behind the madness and it had to shine through all the myriad details of a 3-year Project, because it had worked.

Second, to statistically prove that the Project had made a significant difference across all measured performance metrics, not just as a function of the normal progress of the organization, but in a truly transformative way. This evaluation work was done and approved by all management levels of Apa Nova and Veolia.

Their signature on all the facts and figures sealed the application for the competition. Two months after the submission, on the 6th of November, 2018, the much awaited e-mail arrived: "CONGRATULATIONS!" The application had been accepted into the final phase of the competition, and essentially achieved the goal set out for it 3 years before.

The final round was still to unfold in January, 2019, at the Business Transformation World Summit in Orlando, Florida. The top management team and Advanced Thinking went there and passed a rigorous final evaluation from the panel of judges. Just like in performance sports, 3 years of efforts came down to a few hours of High-Level Leadership and Management performance.

After it was over, there were still a few hours of restless waiting until the final results were presented during the official ceremony. Then, the envelope opened with the rip-roaring news: the Project was selected as the best in the World!

Food for thought:

- How would you measure the success of business transformation in your organization?
- How would you know if it's good enough?

Reach for Synergy: Building a 21ˢᵗ Century Multi-Company Organization

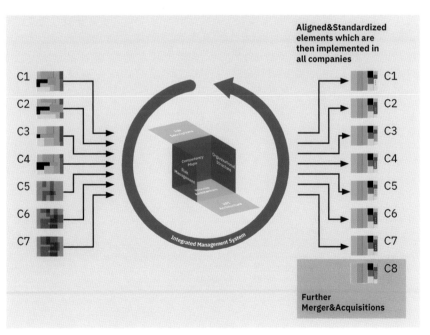

From the very beginning, an overarching desire behind the Reengineering Project was to lay the foundation for an exceptional Country Business Setup across Romania, as an example for the entire Central and Eastern European region and possibly the world.

The plan was to start small, but always with the big picture in mind. The Project management team had to be able to act fast when opportunities arose, to achieve that big goal. The timing was just right. Why? Because the Project was gaining international appreciation, as seen in Chapter 3. The present Chapter is about all the Veolia companies in Romania, and the plan to co-create their future by broadening their vision towards a single country-type, 21st century multi-company organization.

Until January, 2018, the focus had been set on the Reengineering Project, already ongoing for Apa Nova, one of the eight Veolia companies in Romania. The new Process Architecture had already been implemented in Apa Nova, and the company was ready to join hands and create the new Process Architecture – the TO BE phase – with the final tweaks still underway. In time, people understood how a process could start in one structure and cross many others, so they gradually moved from Functional Thinking to Process Thinking. The final TO BE phase at Apa Nova became their AS IS, once this new phase began for all Veolia companies.

The other Veolia companies in Romania benefited from the experience of Apa Nova during this joint effort of transformation. The task was to create a complete picture of their actual processes. All companies gradually came on board, starting with the most representative ones from each business line. The objective was to align, standardize and implement the new way of doing business across all these companies.

Easy to say, but let's see how it was done.

1. Getting All the Veolia Companies in Romania on Board

Change is a natural human process. In order to successfully adapt to change, people need to increase their awareness. Really understanding themselves and others leads to an awareness of reality, their similarities and discrepancies, which is essential for anybody who wants to open up to any kind of real change. This is especially significant, since each Veolia company in Romania had different organizational cultures, different backgrounds and financial status.

A. Rome Wasn't Built in a Day

As you may already expect, a Project of such complexity can't be implemented for all companies at once. Based on a deep analysis of the real state of affairs within each company, the top management team decided to deploy this Reengineering Project gradually. Companies or groups of companies were introduced in the Project at different moments in time, when their availability and power to make a contribution were optimal. Furthermore, it became part of the Veolia strategy for Romania to immediately engage any newly acquired organization in the Reengineering Project.

Based on their resources and capabilities at that time, two companies engaged in the Project at the beginning of 2018, to create the AS IS picture of the Veolia companies in Romania. The beginning was not as smooth as one might expect. The newcomers came with different appetites for change.

Later, the third company who joined the Project faced a difficult internal context. Its General Manager had been replaced only one day before the Project kick-off meeting. Obviously, this had a great impact on everyone. Had you been there, you might have been dumbfounded by the contagious sense of confusion.

The next two companies were invited at a later phase in the Project, during the standardization of the processes. Due to the incredibly fast dynamics of the Reengineering Project, they had to be brought in earlier than initially programmed in the Master Plan. This meant that they had to jump in a bus that was already on the move. Put yourself in their shoes! They hopped in right in the middle of the trip – in the standardization phase. Their challenge was to contribute just as much as their more experienced colleagues from the other companies, while struggling to make up for the time difference. Difficult, isn't it?

But not as difficult as it was for the last company, who entered the Project during the Implementation phase. They had to quickly understand the methodology of the Project, catch-up with all the mapped standard processes, resolve any misalignment with their actual processes, and begin the implementation at the same time as the other companies.

The eighth company was acquired at the end of the Alignment & Standardization phase, and it became the beneficiary of the Organizational Architecture Model that had already been developed.

According to the Master Plan and the thinking direction of the entire Project, the local management teams of these companies had to get familiarized with the methodology. Why? To be able to get on board, to ensure proper communication and engagement right from the beginning, and to set the proper tone from the top. An active support from local management teams is one of the essential factors in creating the optimal environment and motivation for a successful Project.

During these kick-off meetings, the main goal was to get to know the real situation and pain points of each company. But dealing with different companies, each one with its own organizational culture and vision, raised yet another challenge. The strategy to get the local management teams on board had to be adapted, and often the Project management team had to be decisive about initiating the Project inside these companies; there was no turning back from such a decision.

B. Embrace the Differences

During the early meetings with the first three companies, Advanced Thinking studied all the relevant documents for each company: organizational charts, lists of processes, examples of procedures, work instructions, Job Descriptions and any other documents that captured the specificity of every company. As expected, they found different organizational hierarchies, which was a valuable insight in the cultural mindset of each company: control, responsibility or collaboration. Also, the difference in hierarchies revealed that some structures were super-hierarchical and others were flat, even though they provided the same service or product. At the same time, the same structures were allocated on different levels of subordination.

When comparing the practices of the Veolia companies in Romania, it became obvious that there were many discrepancies in people's thinking, acting and relating to each other, both horizontally and vertically throughout the structure of the organization. This showed how departments interacted in every organization: with a stubborn mindset about "how we do things here".

There were also some pretty big differences in the way companies had chosen to document and implement their systems of norms, procedures and work instructions. Some of them kept a very well documented system, others a more liberal one. It revealed much about how a company enforced its rules.

This was a first impression of the similarities and differences among all companies, from an organizational point of view – a snapshot of how work was organized. Afterwards, there were kick-off meetings, knowledge transfer sessions, reviews and other such meetings for each company, in order to obtain the Alignment & Standardization of processes. This created the AS IS picture for each company, and introduced everyone to the methodology of the Project. During these meetings, the Project management team validated everyone's effort and contribution by using everything that had been built in the companies up until then. Nothing was demolished, nothing was denied. This aimed to lay the foundations of a mutual trust relationship, crucial for that kind of endeavor.

However, as with every beginning, some employees had strong reactions against the Reengineering Project. The challenge was to harmonize all kinds of reactions – some expressed, others just implied – which soon crystallized into four types of attitudes. The same way a chameleon is changing its colors to adapt to the situation, the Advanced Thinking team had to adjust their discourse and send the right messages in order to get everyone in the same boat. It was imperative to constantly nurture and maintain the bond with every single member of the Project teams, as you can see in the following examples:

- **The "If it's a must, let's do it…" attitude**

The drastic internal management changes of the third company that joined the Project triggered the "If it's a must, let's do it…" attitude. There was a massive cloud of confusion hanging around. No one knew what to expect from the newly appointed local General Manager. He was undergoing a thorough induction phase, therefore the employees had neither leadership, nor immediate guidance.

In the beginning, people found neither the reason for change nor any incentive to commit to the Project. The company was overwhelmed by the daily operational fire-fighting, trying to react to constant challenges, and so it was naturally paralyzed when faced with the magnitude of change required. The Project was seen as a "must". Nobody had time to think about improvement.

- **The "Why should we do this?" attitude**

Another type of attitude was strongly influenced by one of the local management teams. People – being naturally proud of their results and achievements over time – were overwhelmed by the high volume of work required by the Project, considering that they had already done everything for their company.

Accordingly, there were no resources for the Project, and all employees were already fully involved in daily activities.

The main question was: *"Why should we get involved in something like this? We sincerely believe our company is already performing at its best!"*

People were uneager to begin any transformation at any level of the company, because they believed everything was going great, therefore they neither had time nor reason to get involved.

The kick-off meetings focused on general problems that many organizations face all over the world. One of the most overlooked problems is misplacing the attention on effects rather than on causes. This can happen due to a dynamic business environment which inspires an overstated sense of urgency. Therefore, a company in this situation may overlook non value-added activities, or wastes of any kind embedded in its processes.

The local management team was reassured that their previous efforts and results were highly appreciated, nothing had been in vain and all their work would be useful to the Project. Slowly, the attitude changed, and people eventually embraced the vision of the Project.

• **The "To do or not to do this?" attitude**
Another type of attitude was a downright paradox. Even though the local management team was disengaged and unconvinced by the benefits of the Project, the employees who were directly involved in the transformation process fully committed to sharing their knowledge and expertise.

Although trained to work and act responsibly, without support from their local management team, some of the people involved in the Project were skeptical at first, and reluctant to share their opinions. However, as they were constantly asked for their input and appreciated during meetings, they eventually became more open to share their clarity and fresh perspective.

• **The "We have to do this!" attitude**
This is the attitude of a company that was in an uncertain situation because it was negotiating the extension of its concession contract. They too were aware of the efforts required by the Reengineering Project. However, they were confident that there was no place to go but up, and they embarked on a long and deep transformation despite the possibility that all their work could have been in vain. They actively participated in meetings, determined to share their experience, ideas and vision, while "back home" their labor contracts were pending termination.

The positive attitude of the local General Manager, backed by the commitment of his team, encouraged the employees to remain fully involved throughout the Project.

How Was All of This Possible?

Advanced Thinking developed a consistent communication strategy to help people adopt a mobilizing sense of urgency, to understand and embrace the mission and vision of the Reengineering Project. That was a crucial turning point where three layers of centered focus had to be simultaneously integrated: merging the **organizational cultures** with the **methodological frame** and with the **timeline** of the Group's Global Strategy – One Veolia Objective.

What would the next reasonable step be, keeping in mind what you already know from Chapter 2? Isn't it all about seeing the AS IS state first?

2. How to Take a Relevant HD Picture of Reality

As in the case of Apa Nova, the first goal was the full understanding and mapping of the work done in the Veolia companies that had recently joined the Project. An accurate image of their current situation – the AS IS state – was the basis for the Reengineering of every piece of work done in all the companies, so as to reach an optimized Process Architecture – the TO BE state – at country level.

The first challenge was to get people to overcome their belief that the Reengineering Project meant nothing more than another restructuring initiative. Think about it: in the last 20 years, there had been many waves of restructuring, all bearing fancy names, and all **just modifying** structures from the organizational chart. The consequence was that hundreds of positions were restructured after each wave.

Their attitude changed when everybody eventually understood that they were taking part in a Business Transformation Project through Reengineering, which was nothing like restructuring. Surprise-surprise: unlike all previous experiences, this time people were invited to look at the processes and capture every single activity and every single role within each process, careful not to leave anyone out. Everyone and everything was taken into consideration, including the work of each manager's assistant, courier or archivist. **No one was left behind.**

The Project teams had to use the same Process Mapping Standard as detailed in Chapter 2. That meant they had to map their daily work in a timely

order, using elements like activities, roles, deliverables and performance indicators. It took quite a while for all the teams to calibrate with each other and
achieve the optimal granularity of their process descriptions.

From the very first iterations of the process mapping, it became obvious
that some activities were left out. Funny as it may seem, many of the missing
roles belonged to the managers. Take a look at the questions below and see
what the answers reveal:

"Can the process go on without a manager approving the document?"
"No, without the approval of the manager, we cannot continue."

"Then why didn't you map the manager's role within the process?"
"Oh, we wouldn't dare to impose."

By constantly asking: *"What else does this person do in order to provide the delivera-*
ble?"; *"What is the next activity in the process?"* and *"What else needs to be done?"*, the
teams finally began to find the right outline of their processes.

Contrastingly, there was a tendency to describe some of the daily activities
that people performed and which did not appear to really belong to the process
under discussion. The explanation went along these lines: *"But I am also doing*
this", or *"I used to do this every time I finished this activity because I was asked to do so*
by that department."

The Advanced Thinking team went back to the methodology to remind
everybody what a stakeholder was, what triggered a process, when a process
started and when it ended, what the business object of a process was, and so
on. Questions like: *"Is this activity mandatory to fulfil the stakeholder's request?"*;
"Which stakeholder/who needs the outcome of this activity?"; *"Can the process continue*
without this activity?" were paramount. People discovered that sometimes, activities requested by some stakeholders were embedded by design in a process
started by another stakeholder. Other times, there were some activities which
didn't belong to the process in question, but to other processes, mapped by a
different team.

To really understand why this happened, let's remember the mindset that
people had in the beginning of the Project. They thought that the Project was all
about restructuring, so they wanted to show off their workload and how indis-
pensable they were. They feared their everyday work would not be visible to
the top management team anymore, so you could often hear *"But I am the one*
who performs this work, not him! Why shouldn't I map this activity?"

It was a challenge at that time to get people out of a mindset constricted by departmental boundaries and functions. They had to remember that a role is a type of person having the necessary skills, knowledge and abilities to perform one or more specific activities, and that a process is a sum of roles performed regardless of the Organizational Structures.

Gradually, people realized that each person can perform multiple roles in multiple processes. But that doesn't necessarily mean that the structures these people work in own these processes. **Step by step, the feeling of belonging to one department or another began to fade, while the feeling of belonging to one process or another grew.**

Over time, people's expertise developed as they became continuously involved in the Project. Consequently, knowledge transfer was tailored according to the participants' level of understanding, using the principle of Standard Process Fragments.

The participants were constantly encouraged to present their process maps to each other. During such meetings, they realized that sequences of identical activities were mapped in different processes, in different words. The logical inference was that either the ownership of the process fragments was incorrectly allocated or that more people were doing the same set of activities in different processes. If the latter was true, the same activities would have been described redundantly.

The solution was to standardize those process fragments. A standard process fragment represents a sequence of activities which are repeated more than once in the same process or in different processes. This revolutionized process mapping and changed the mentality again. For example, the secretarial activities, the document registration activities, the training activities, etc. were considered Standard Process Fragments.

As the "joining hands" type of meetings continued with everyone involved in the Project, people discovered the real process boundaries. Finally sitting at the same table, they got to the real start and end of the processes, shattered the walls between structures, removed redundant activities, and discovered areas with an unclear allocation of responsibility.

In the beginning, when they were asked *"where and when should this activity be done?"* the answer was:

> *"This can be done here or there, in one way or another, the most important thing is to get it done."*
> *"And who is responsible for doing this?"*

"Somebody from one of the structures!"
"But who exactly?"
"Somebody must be!"

Unfortunately, when **anybody** or **somebody** is responsible, in fact **nobody** is. Ultimately, the teams placed the responsibility correctly, pinpointing what **role** was responsible for a certain activity.

People were overwhelmed by having to perform their daily duties at the same time as being involved in the Reengineering Project. They were eager to see their work done and all the processes mapped. Some of them looked for the easy way out by "borrowing" the Process Maps from Apa Nova. Some of them oversimplified their work – the common mistake of combining multiple roles into a single one. This was a twisted interpretation of high level process mapping. As one member of the Project management team expressed it, *"You can't see the tourist sites on a map if you don't use the proper scale."* But soon all of them learned that jumping the line was not a viable solution; it was only self-deceit. Instead of getting caught up in "how they did it at Apa Nova", they bit the bullet and mapped the processes as they were.

Step by step and by working hard daily, the companies involved in the Project finished mapping the AS IS picture. The results were presented in reviews, highlighting and emphasizing the clarity obtained after this massive effort. Each review could tell its own story as the knowledge and awareness of the Project teams evolved, increasing organizational maturity.

However, the deadlines of daily tasks became difficult to meet because of this constant strife for agreement on the sequence of activities. Solid tension or deep relaxation were common feelings during reviews. There were times when one felt stuck and pressured, or cheerful and colorful as a rainbow. Regardless of the situation, the emotional state travelled in the room like an obsessive sneeze, at the speed of light.

Memorable phrases and moments during the meetings were ingrained in the DNA of the Project. One day, someone said, with a drained expression:

"I am so tired, I haven't slept in almost a week! The voice of the process kept me up all night!"

Another unforgettable moment was when people presented the status they
achieved between reviews to the Project management team: *"Our sponsor has already prepared a plaque for you with your name on it for all the hard work you've done so far"*, said a manager in an amusing way. It emphasized the fact that these reviews were not meant to keep an eye on people's work, but to get a grasp of the status-quo and progress gained at every step in the Project.

During some reviews where some people kept complaining about how difficult it was to map their work, one question appeared on the tip of everyone's tongue. At some point, a member of the top management team asked it:

"If you say you know what you are doing and that all your processes are accurately reflected by the procedures, then why did you have to work so hard on this?"

The reply touched on the heart of the matter:

"Our processes were already documented, but not like this. It took us a while to understand the benefits of this new way of mapping; we really needed to change our thinking around the concept of Role and the responsibility associated with the process role."

It's true that some companies had mapped their processes according to the Process Mapping Standard much more accurately than others, due to a continuous pressure from the local management team to do the right things right. That was highly appreciated by the Project management team and was given as an example to all the Veolia companies in Romania.

During one meeting, someone from the Project management team emphasized:

"90% of people know what to do, 60% know how to do it, and only 10% of them know why we do what we do."

As people worked, they began to see the bigger picture that explained *why they do what they do every day*. Moreover, they discovered what others do day-to-day, and got rid of the feeling that *"I am working my socks off and they mess around wasting their time."*

Another win came from the sheer participation in review meetings. Having to present their work, people polished their presentation skills from one meeting to another. Some Project teams had a real problem with showing their entire work printed on endless sheets of paper, but one member of the Project management team explained that *"the purpose of this presentation is not to show how much we worked, but to prove that we understood what we do."*

The Project management team was on the look out for signs that could confirm that everyone involved properly integrated the principles and essence of the methodology, and also that they found a successful way to replicate it. After such revelations, the emotional state in the room transformed into a prevalent sense of admiration for the new way of thinking.

Some of the people involved in the Project were always two steps ahead, thinking fast and expanding their knowledge, being inquisitive and asking bold questions. For instance, at the end of the Process Mapping phase, some began to wonder: *"fine, we mapped our processes, but shouldn't we know how much time and money these processes actually require?"* That was one of the many marvelous moments of insight, when people anticipated what would happen next in the Project.

As mentioned in previous chapters, meetings were not swamped in ideological theories, but directly connected with everyday reality. People left these meetings with guidance and practical improvement tips. Some ideas were brought by the Project management team from their previous experience in the Project: *"in Apa Nova, we used to do a lot of pointless checking. How many eyes do you think are necessary to check one document?"*

Managers were asked a lot of questions, to establish how they saw their daily activities: *"Do you like examining all incoming documents in your company? Why should all contract requests be sent to the manager?"* The answer – *"because I must check if something is missing"* – reveals the fact that there is considerable room for improvement.

In the same spirit, there were questions like: *"if it's a simple request, is it OK for the paper to go through the entire organization?"* By receiving answers like: *"it only takes one day for it to go through the organization. This shouldn't be too long for the customer!"* people discovered the need for more insight into value-added activities and associated KPIs. So, at the operational level, people were realizing that responsibility shouldn't be set randomly, but it should be indicated by the process flow.

To wrap it up, the discussion slowly slipped to the area of potential improvements for the existing processes, emphasizing the need for change. During meetings, new and old ideas popped out in a frenzy, like popcorn. Old ideas that had not been accepted previously, managed to find the nurturing ground to sprout. Looking at the mapped processes, people could clearly see new ways of doing their work, from a fresh perspective. There were moments of revelation and joy; it was like springtime.

Looking back at the end of the AS IS phase, the messages received from the Project teams were invaluable signs of the true success of our endeavor. If you compiled the feedback across the Veolia companies in Romania, you would find this:

> *"I never participated in something similar to this before, nor did I think it could be done this way. We tried to involve as many people as we could. The communication between us clearly improved. We'd gone through (improvement) projects in the past, but nothing like this. For me, this was very good. We were taken out of our comfort zone, and everything really is better. We now have an accurate image of what we are doing, and some of us finally understood what our colleagues do every day."*

Questions addressed to different people from different companies, like: *"Do you think recruiting should be different from one Veolia company to another?"* received a unanimous answer: *"Recruiting should be the same. There's no reason for it to be different, given the fact that the internal needs and legal standards are the same in every company."*

> *"How about invoicing a service, measuring the customer's satisfaction, assuring the Integrated Management System, etc.?"*

> *"They should be the same, no matter the company."*

Throughout the Project, the Union Leaders were invited to meetings alongside everyone. One of them said: *"Aha, now I get it! So, isn't it true that the next step is identifying the identical processes across all companies, negotiating, agreeing and then putting them into practice in the same way?"*

Apart from the personal contribution to mapping the work, the Project management team hoped to ensure that a sincere mass communication about the Reengineering Project would come through the voice of the Union Leaders.

After finishing their AS IS picture, the multi-company process teams had to gather around the same table and to align and standardize the best version of their processes.

3. Synergy of Best Practice: Replication of Methodology

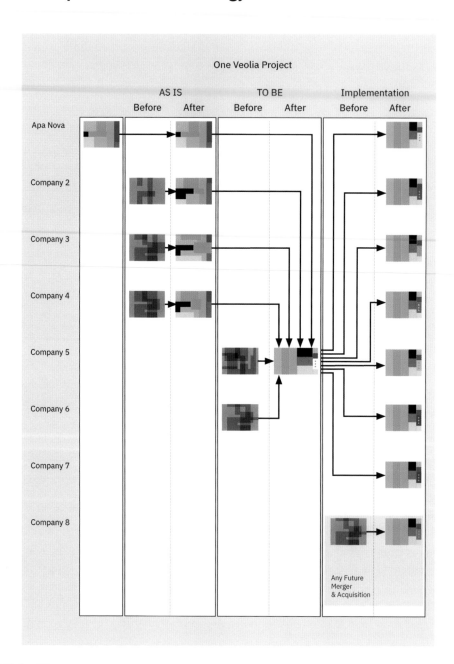

Let's take one step back and remember the vision of a Project to create a multi-company 21st century organization. Right from the beginning, it was clear
that the foundation for such an Organizational Architecture in a multi-company, at country level, should be laid on common grounds between all the
companies participating in the Reengineering effort. The newly envisioned
Organizational Architecture should promote mutual benefits for each of the
companies adopting it. Naturally, one word came to mind, to perfectly describe
that vision: **synergy.**

Generally defined as *"an interaction of elements that, when combined, produce a
total effect which is greater than the sum of the individual elements, contributions, etc.",*
synergy became the goal to strive for. The phase of Aligning & Standardizing
processes from all Veolia companies in Romania started in mid-2018. In line
with the Group's Global Strategy – One Veolia Objective, this phase was intended
to lay the foundation of an exceptional Country Business Setup capable to continuously exceed all stakeholder expectations.

As mentioned before, one of the principles that guided the previous AS
IS phase when mapping the daily work, was to show respect for what had
already been built in all those companies, thus recognizing and promoting
their best practices.

Now let's reflect a little on what had already been done. All the companies
had already mapped their activities by applying the same methodology, meaning
they had a common knowledge base and a common, process-focused thinking.

**In fact, the vision of a modern multi-company organization can be
described as a synergetic implementation of best practices through a repli-
cation of methodology across all the companies it includes. Applying the same
methodology leads to an integrated Process Architecture design. This creates
the premises for aligning all other organizational elements.**

Even though the plan for the Alignment & Standardization phase of the
Project seemed relatively clear and straightforward, many bridges had to be
crossed. One of the most difficult obstacles to overcome was that there were no
two companies alike. As previously described (Chapter 4.1.B), all companies
had very different organizational cultures, structures, specific activities related
to different business lines, and so on. All these differences were clearly visible
when comparing their AS IS process maps.

The standardization and alignment of the Process Architecture was done
in two steps: first, selecting the obvious processes that could be aligned immediately among all companies. Some of the examples are Human Resources,
Financial and IT, and generally supporting processes. Thus, 14 process groups

were formed and categorized by their internal or external stakeholder. Second, once the obvious processes were aligned and standardized, it became possible to start looking at other processes as well. When paying closer attention, activities related to maintenance work, concession contracts, and operational activities could also be aligned and standardized across companies.

A. Building the Foundation of Our Common Future

The question that followed intuitively was: *„how to manage people and achieve synergy, when they come from different companies, different organizational cultures, and have different levels of will and competence?"*

A Crystal-Clear Methodology Is Gold

In order to facilitate the first discussions regarding the Alignment & Standardization phase at country level, the management of each company had to propose a coordinator for each process group. From these proposals, the top management team selected the most suitable people to become process group coordinators, at country level. However, the "why should we do this?" attitude is one of the real difficulties of this type of Project: even though the requirements for nominating a coordinator were clear, there was a company that did not put forward any proposal at all, being consistent with this kind of attitude.

The majority of the appointed process group coordinators were part of the staff at Apa Nova, mainly due to their previous experience in designing a new Process Architecture (the TO BE phase, already designed for Apa Nova at that time). However, there were two process groups in which the appointed coordinators came from the other Veolia companies in Romania, as recognition for their engagement in and contribution to the Project.

Next, each process group coordinator received the task of appointing a deputy coordinator and assembling a cross-companies Project team. The coordinators had the liberty to appoint any deputy they considered, from any company, to contribute in a valuable way. As a result, they chose deputies that complemented their know-how of the processes under their responsibility. Employees from each company had to be part of the Project teams, bringing relevant and useful knowledge on the specificities of their processes.

After all the Project teams had been assembled and obtained the approval of the Project management team, they needed a framework to assist and guide them. In this respect, the Project management team created a cloud-based workspace to be used by every process group team. This collaborative workspace facilitated communication, guaranteeing a high degree of visibility and transparency for everybody involved in the Project: they shared calendars, documents, as well as important communication/information. Everybody saw everything!

Not all of them made use of that, though. Some process groups had a slow start, since people failed to prepare beforehand and to study any document other than their own. Even so, the strong commitment to transparency was intended as a constant reminder that all this endeavor had always been about **teamwork**, and the objective was to design a common Process Architecture for all companies.

Studying each other's work was a prerequisite of paramount importance for all the following steps. Apa Nova was a step ahead of all other companies, having already mapped its TO BE processes. But in order to have a common foundation for a single Process Architecture, the Project teams considered the TO BE processes of Apa Nova as any other AS IS. By doing that, all the companies had the same position from the very beginning; it was a powerful message that they would all be considered equal at the starting line. They reassured everybody that no idea, strategy or decision would be imposed by Apa Nova.

The progress within the Alignment & Standardization was sustained through periodical meetings followed by monthly reviews, to keep the Project management team updated. Every representative from each company had to present the AS IS processes. Then, the whole team had to analyze and identify all the best practices.

This was the "Synergetic Engine", or how processes were designed with inputs from all companies. Process group coordinators were asked to keep a record of all discussions and decisions taken during the meetings. In this way, a traceability of inputs from every participant was available at any time and was meant to make them responsible for the decisions taken. Nonetheless, not everybody was equally committed.

After all nominalizations had been made, everybody was invited to a larger meeting. This first meeting set the scene for the next step of the Project. It made it official and restated the sheer need to commit to what would come next, allowing newcomers to feel comfortable and openly begin their Journey.

Anticipating possible objections in the room – due to previous experience – one of the members of the Project management team "predicted":

"You will find that some people are overloaded and others have lighter loads to bear. The TO BE will be as performant as you envision it. It will be sustained

by your organization because it will be the result of your decisions. You will not be influenced by anybody from Apa Nova."

Hearing this statement once more felt like melting another block of the "resistance to change" attitude and the room got a degree warmer. Then, projecting the future and getting rid of more fear and resistance, the person continued:

> *"The TO BE **phase** must be ready as soon as possible, to enable the Continuous Improvement projects, using Lean Six Sigma methodology. Improvement doesn't mean restructuring. It means decreasing the waiting time, reducing costs, improving the work environment, and much more for our stakeholders."*

The dialog in the room became lighter and more familiar, as members from Apa Nova shared insights about the gains and losses they had during the two years of experience in the Project: *"With endless resources, any fool can manage! The wisest thing would be to achieve the maximum benefits with the existing resources and at the right pace. What's more, we designed a clear Process Architecture with our people, for our people"*; *"in 2017 vs 2016, there is 30% less overtime at Apa Nova, while increasing the network efficiency, and decreasing the consumption. Now we decreased the excessive paperwork through digitalization."*

During these intense few hours, many people understood and accepted the mindset of the Project to different degrees. They went back to their organization filled with motivation and energy, like trains gathering at the central station, and then each spread back to their designated destination. Others failed to change their initial attitude and continued to express their distrust and fear throughout the Project. This had to be constantly managed and addressed within the Project teams.

The methodology itself seemed easy, compared to what was by far the most challenging aspect within the Project: some people's pride of having the best processes, and their fear of having technical solutions imposed by other companies.

There's No Achievement Without Hard Work

As a first step, the members of each process group identified the "equivalent" processes in all companies, no matter how these processes were named. It was time to understand the methodology better. After process equivalence, the next step was to check and agree on the process start and end. To that purpose, the Project management team developed a process identification template which

could easily guide anybody at that point. A very important role was played by
the process group coordinators, who had previous experience and understanding of the Project and who were also promoters within their teams.

The Project teams had to clearly document the start of every process: a unique combination of the origin of the entry (the stakeholder), its request and the first activity in the process.

The next step was to document the end of the process: also a unique combination of the last activity in the process, deliverables and the destination of the outputs. This trio also gained another function, which was to align people's understanding of what triggers a process and which are its deliverables. Another eye-opener provided by the methodology was understanding that the process ends when all requests from all stakeholders are satisfied.

As expected, the start and/or the end of a process was sometimes different from what people had thought before. A lot of heated discussions took place around what some of the companies initially called a "Close utilities contract" process. After everybody presented their situation, the process group team realized that, for some of the companies, this process started with a request to design the new network connection. For other companies, it started with the request to install that network, and, for others, it started with just the request to turn on the utilities on an existing network connection. This implied totally different scopes to the process. The teams realized that there were three distinct requests that could be placed by the customer, consequently triggering three distinct processes.

Process group teams met whenever necessary and monthly reviews were organized so that the Project management team could get updates on the status of the Project. The coordinators received feedback and questions that opened up new perspectives about the work they did in every process group. Those reviews were one of the most important pillars of the Alignment & Standardization phase.

During one review meeting, the Environment process group coordinator raised the problem of how to map a process that could be standardized across multiple process groups at country level. The name of the process was "Create reports". The idea came like a lightning strike to most of the coordinators, because they realized that most of them didn't map this process, even though this kind of activity took a lot out of everyone's time. It was a long debate about how specifically this kind of process should be mapped.

During another review, the Customer process group coordinator – an employee of Apa Nova – enthusiastically informed the Project management team that his team decided to adopt some of the best practices from another company, as they were "more flexible". This showed how everyone took into account ideas from the other companies involved.

Moreover, the Project management team acted as the voice of the Process Mapping Standard, constantly reminding people several things: to pay attention to the granularity of process maps, to identify all the stakeholders for each process, and to identify the processes from the very first input to the very last output at company level.

The next task in the Project was to identify similar activities in a process, which are named differently in each company, and to align the vocabulary. Visualize a situation in which the exact same activity was defined by another verb ("Dig the pit" vs "Perform the dig") or the same verb depicted other kinds of activity ("Repair the defect" – for a pipe vs "Repair the defect" – for an IT application). Can you imagine how complicated this kind of exercise can get? However, doing it always pays off.

Soon, another important fact was observed: similar processes seemed different from one company to another, due to technological misalignment, including IT. Hence, everybody needed to keep to the rule of technology-free mapping. **They were constantly reminded to map their activities in such a way that technology could not make a difference in how they described the process. The mapping needed to capture the "what" of each activity, not "how" it was performed. They were advised to use work instructions to describe in detail technology-driven activities, when appropriate.**

After the processes were aligned, possible technological solutions (like the general use of a software for maintenance, fleet management applications and the introduction of tablets at operational level) became a topic for debate among team members. It felt like people discovered the natural order of things: **first build a robust process that details what needs to be done and only afterwards hold debates about how technology (not only IT) can help that process.**

In reviews, there were moments when some could speak in front of everyone and felt free to unburden themselves:

"Yes, my team and I admit that it was difficult to understand each other and to find common ground."

Soon after, somebody else would be saying: *"you're not the only one, I felt like that, too."* Those kinds of moments brought everyone closer; nobody was alone in the turmoil of that Journey. Process group coordinators also shared the valuable moments when they managed to reach consensus within teams. That was another way of sharing best practices – best practices in cooperating, even though participants were from different companies and cities, yet all members of the Reengineering Project.

There were also precious tips & tricks that the top management team gave to process group coordinators during those reviews. They were really paying attention to every detail presented by the process group coordinators, not only to ensure that the Project followed the Master Plan, but also to truly challenge the Project teams to go beyond the traditional vision of their processes. For example, one member of the top management team challenged the Human Resources and Acquisition process group with the next question:

"How should some activities related to hiring people be different from those related to purchasing any other type of resources?"

In these types of projects, messages can sometimes be confusing. At one point, people thought that there were too many identified processes and that they should somehow be merged. That was reason enough for the Project teams' members to discard the rules of properly identifying processes, which were clearly stated by the methodology. The teams ended up spending a lot of time trying to resolve these two conflicting inputs.

People's understanding of the fundamental principles behind this Project grew steadily. This led to process maps improving in time. Often, the Project management team cheered the process group teams for their efforts and hard work. In the end, one thing is essential: all the Project teams managed to accomplish the remarkable performance of completing the TO BE process mapping with one and a half months before the deadline set by the Project management team.

Spreading the Knowledge at the Right Time and Pace

At that time in the Alignment & Standardization phase of the Project, the teams had to identify the important control points, so as to assess performance inside of a process as well as at the end of the process, to make sure that the requirements of the stakeholder were properly met. What are the most useful and important control points that impact the highest level of decision-making?

Let's start by defining that "highest level". If we refer to a single company, everything seems clear enough, but how about a multi-company country organization? It became obvious that in order to even have this discussion during the meetings, it was necessary for every person involved in the Project to achieve a common knowledge base: from what a KPI actually represents, to how to design and how to enable data-driven decision-making.

So, companies that needed a knowledge update received various trainings. These trainings were more than plain knowledge transfers. They included actual case studies (previously developed at Apa Nova) to exemplify every theoretical concept.

Having so many different organizations around the table, it became clear enough that this was a good moment to start designing and standardizing the performance indicators for all process groups, so the development of a multi-company integrated Architecture of Key Performance Indicators began.

As a consequence, two types of generic KPIs were defined for the following categories: Quality, Cost and Delivery Time. Then followed a discussion with all the coordinators of the process groups, in order to explain and further refine the KPI Architecture.

When referring to Quality Performance Indicators, it is of utmost importance to underline two aspects: correctness and completeness, because, no matter the activity, the deliverable must be both complete and correct in relation to what is requested of it. You probably wouldn't buy a smartphone without a screen or with dysfunctional circuits, would you?

The Delivery Time Performance Indicators have two main aspects: Total Time (i.e., Lead Time, the necessary time from receiving a request until delivering the requested product or service to the customer) and Actual Work Time (known as Cycle Time, the time spent to actually execute an activity without waiting or preparation times).

For sure, the customer's expectation is to receive what he/she requested and when he/she requested it, but it's in the interest of the business to know exactly how much time it takes to deliver, because, as we all know, time is money!

And when it comes to money, one could find it difficult to think about cost as a measure of one's process performance. The Project teams' members were asked to define a performance indicator for the cost of their process. That was really difficult in the beginning, and naturally the costs that first came to mind for their processes were those generated by unfulfilling the stakeholders' requests (something like penalties due to delays).

From this point of view, there were two important aspects to the Cost-related Performance Indicators: Actual Cost – we had to know how much we spent for an activity, so as to compare it with how much we budgeted for this activity – and Cost of Poor Quality.

Cost of Poor Quality was a new concept for the companies, yet again a new way of looking at things. Everybody acknowledges the fact that even scrap has a cost of its own. But apart from all the costs "felt" and registered by the Financial department (inspections, warranty, rejects, penalties, etc.), there are many other "hidden" costs, like sales compromises, long cycle times, excessive set-ups, lost sales, overtime, excess inventory, and so on, not to mention employee morale. And what about rework? Is the duration of rework measured? By rework, we refer to repeated activities caused by the fact that they're not done right the first time. This represents a gold mine for Continuous Improvement initiatives: future Lean Six Sigma improvement projects.

Actual Cost seemed to be a clearer concept, but when we wanted to compare it with the budgeted cost, we knew that "*the budgets are not process-based; at the lowest level, they are structure-related*", as one of the managers said. This generated a fragmented view of costs. And that was a new challenge: to redesign the budgeting process to match the new Process Architecture.

When asked what the cost of executing a process was, people couldn't give a straight answer. In fact, they said they neither had a way to measure it, nor to input available data. Even the members of the financial process group feared that it was not possible to estimate the cost of their processes. The coordinator of this process group replied:

> "*If the financial process group cannot be a good example for all the others, then who can?*"

A guideline for what, where and how to measure performance indicators was developed, so anyone, from any Veolia company in Romania, could align and measure the process KPIs in a similar manner. That created the premises for a coherent and integrated Dashboard at country level.

But having a unique KPI Architecture implemented in all companies didn't mean having the same targets. These should be relevant for each company and must be adapted to the reality of each one, meaning business line, specific activities, financial profile, and top-down decisions.

In order to promote a data-driven management, the first thing to do would be to make use of the data collected in process control points. A statistical approach is the best way to do this, and this is where all the extensive knowledge of data analysis comes in handy. Even a member of the Project management team emphasized this during one of the review sessions:

"You have piles of data! You are all managers, so use that data. We are a nation of philosophers! Let's talk less and do more."

That was in fact an invitation for everyone to shift towards a data-driven decision-making mindset, to find the essential information and to avoid redundancy.

The greatest advantage of implementing a single approach in measuring the performance of aligned and standardized processes across all companies is that KPIs can be consolidated in a single multi-company dashboard for the use of top management. This offers a real-time, dynamic and integrated overview of the performance of the companies, country-wide.

One Risk to Rule Them All

Now that we discussed about how the KPI Architecture was adapted at country level, let's take a look at Risk Management and how a unique risk culture had to be implemented in all companies. As already detailed in Chapter 2, the methodology used in the Risk Management process was FMEA, already implemented in Apa Nova. Knowledge transfer was mandatory to all other companies, as in the case of data analysis. So, FMEA trainings were delivered in all companies to set a common risk-knowledge base, vocabulary and culture.

OK, mission accomplished, right? Not quite. It's not enough to replicate a Risk Management methodology from one company to another; the key to success would be to adapt the Risk Management tools to the company, and then to address all specific needs of all the companies, at country level.

The most noticeable need for change came from the financial perspective on the Severity assessment scale. Imagine what a loss of 1 million euros could mean for a company with a turnover of 200 million euros, and what impact that could have on a company with a 20 million euros turnover. Big difference, isn't it? In order to obtain a single unitary Risk Management process, applicable to all companies, the assessment scales will have to be revised. To do so, the necessary knowledge transfer in all companies has already been done.

With the FMEA Risk Management methodology implemented at country level, all the organizational elements required for a successful Process Architecture will be integrated. Incorporating a unique Risk Management methodology in all Veolia companies in Romania can definitely be considered one of the most important achievements of the Reengineering Project.

The implementation of a single Risk Management toolkit, adapted to the specific needs of each company, is a giant step forward. This means that different risks from different structures and even different companies can now be included in a single risk mitigation strategy, at country level. This translates into a unitary Risk Management, a more efficient resource allocation for address- ing risk effects and an updated risk appetite, consolidated at the highest level of decision-making.

Once the FMEA template was integrated in a unique procedure for assessing risk, it's been used in all risk assessments across all processes from every company. This provided the opportunity for evaluating process risks from a multi-company perspective, as well as considering different business lines. The result is that more risks will be identified and visualized in the same document, and will be assessed according to the same measurement system. Once fully implemented, FMEA will become fundamental to all the Continuous Improvement processes.

Driving on The Fast Lane, Powered by Technology

One of Veolia's worldwide strategies at that time was Finance in Motion – Finance Transformation. The main objective was to improve the performance of its finance processes. Part of it meant transposing processes into a unique Enterprise Resources Planning (ERP) solution, implemented throughout all companies at country level.

This implied the transition towards a single Finance transactional system, considered as a solution for a leaner and more compliant finance function integration. In order to properly communicate and execute the strategy, Veolia devised a Finance Transformation Plan, with clear responsibilities, implementation timeframe and KPIs set for CFOs, at all levels of decision-making. Having clear objectives assigned to them, the top management team in Romania fully aligned with the Group's strategy and decided on the implementation of a single ERP solution throughout all Veolia companies in Romania. That decision was one of the biggest challenges of the Reengineering Project, and the Project management team constantly tried to turn it into an opportunity.

Technology, including IT, should help processes achieve their goals through automation, thus improving speed, accuracy and reliability of activities. It was a constant mantra that technology might "help" people do wrong things faster or break an existing balanced resource allocation.

Let's take a donut shop for example: is it really a good idea to install a super performant portioning machine without having a significant increase in product demand? This could affect the process balance, making all the other activities, downstream and upstream, seem as if they are underperforming. Problems like waiting, bottlenecks, excessive work in progress and uneven workload could occur if the contribution of technology was not integrated within the whole process and linked with its targets.

Two important decisions had to be taken in order to increase the impact of Veolia's strategy to standardize the use of ERP tools across all companies in Romania through the Reengineering Project.

The first one was to link the ERP implementation project with the Alignment & Standardization strategy. The top management team decided to postpone the implementation of ERP solutions across companies for a few months, in order to start with the creation of a common Process Architecture through the Alignment & Standardization phase. This set the premises for a leaner software implementation.

The second decision was to involve, as much as possible, the same people in both the IT implementation and the Alignment & Standardization. The same people were nominated as coordinators for the Alignment & Standardization process group teams, as well as coordinators for the ERP implementation project. By eliminating long and useless communication flows between projects, decision-making became more integrated and synchronized.

Moreover, having the same people in both Project teams meant that the IT implementation team could benefit from the knowledge of the people designing the processes. In a similar way, people designing the processes could communicate in real time all the necessary specifications to the IT implementation team, as their processes were further developing. In fact, this permanent communication between Project teams offered valuable input for both teams and their work.

Of course, there were times when resources seemed insufficient for both the IT project and the Reengineering Project, as they were ongoing at the same time. People felt a bigger pressure on their shoulders, but given the circumstances, the overview from both standpoints helped with the integration of technological components into the processes.

Like the standardization of IT applications, the optimization of management systems initially started separately, in each company, but it was slowly integrated into the Project. Once the Alignment & Standardization phase was completed, the natural step was to implement a unique, integrated, hierarchical and unitary management system. Up to this point, this setup had been independent within each company. Each of the companies had different departments and methods to treat the same – or similar – management system requirements.

One noteworthy change was integrating all the requirements of the reference standards of the management systems adopted by every company, to ensure compliance in an integrated way (for example: ISO 9001, ISO 14001, ISO 17025 and others) and to assign them to a single process. Now, there was a single internal audit team for the Veolia companies in Romania, based on a single set of documents (which integrates ALL requirements), who would perform a single integrated audit, which certified compliance with all standards of requirement.

The necessary activities for the Implementation phase of the Integrated Management System began for the Veolia companies in Romania in July, 2018. The overall objective of this phase was implementation and, of course, its certification. In order to achieve this objective, several intermediate steps had to be carried out.

First of all, an integrated documentation system had to be created. All the procedures had to be not only aligned, but also made applicable to all the business lines of the companies within the Reengineering Project. The Project management team developed a dedicated multi-company team to discuss this step. The team was composed of technical people, consultants, representatives of management systems and others involved in the Continuous Improvement process. As a basic rule, the process teams understood that it would be absolutely logical for one process to have only one procedure.

The strategy and detailed plan for the gradual transition to an Integrated Management System was established. Questions about a proper management system for the multi-company setup popped up again:

- What information do we document and in what kind of document?
- What templates do we use when documenting?
- Who is the owner of each kind of document?
- What is the document hierarchy and what is the connection between the levels of these documents (from the macro to the micro level)?

The teams involved in Alignment & Standardization developed draft documents to provide answers to the questions above and asked process group coordinators to come up with proposals. As a result, some of the process group coordinators came back with a series of rules regarding the process documentation strategy. Those ideas were discussed in several meetings.

The conclusion was that a correct strategy for approaching the documentation system would be the one focused on two major directions. Firstly, it would focus on documenting business rules at different granularity levels such as country, business line, each company, process groups and processes. Secondly, it would document the processes that involved the legal aspects of the operation of the designed processes, based on the rules of the business.

The whole Project management team agreed that the implementation was quite complex, represented a substantial change for the Romanian Veolia companies and had to be adopted gradually, depending on all the restrictive factors (certification milestones, progress in aligning processes, maturity of understanding within the organizations, etc.). The proposal was to immediately adopt only those ideas that could be easily and quickly put into practice by the majority of those involved, and to prepare the second phase for the certification/recertification audit of 2019.

Unique Codification of Documents in the Romanian Veolia Companies

Based on the Process Architecture validated within the Reengineering Project, the final step in designing an Integrated Management System was the development of a unique codification system, at country level.

Once the standardized documents at country level were developed, they were handed over to the Integrated Management System department. These elements and the links between them had to be easy to find and follow. As a result, an efficient coding system was necessary to ensure document traceability.

Correct traceability is obtained when one can link the process group with its processes, the process with its process roles, process roles with their activities and any associated deliverables and role KPIs, for every hand-off. Any form or template used in the execution of any activity within any process needs the same type of linkage.

In other words, once the digitalization of all documents is put into place, anyone can easily identify what he/she has to do, in what process, how to do it, what forms to complete, what is required of him/her and what rules and policies govern his/her activity. A codification system to capture this entire logic had to be implemented.

B. From Theory to Practice

The purpose of all the work submitted so far was aimed to reach a consensus regarding the future way of working, applicable to all companies involved in the Project. It was a difficult but, at the same time, a beautiful journey to put all the perspectives and visions of the Project teams' members in a unique form of standardized and aligned processes for all Veolia companies in Romania. The

Project had come a long way, but still had much to accomplish. So, what next? To put into practice everything that had been realized up until then: to implement the TO BE processes.

In this regard, the Project management team announced the start of the TO BE Implementation phase, as well as its requirements. The implementation time frame was set for 6 months, which was considered enough to adjust or make the final tune-up to the processes.

Before starting work on the Implementation phase, a structured work frame with guidelines set a common way of working for all companies. The local general managers of each company were asked to appoint Implementation Project managers. Each local Implementation Project manager was asked to appoint members for the Implementation teams. The Advanced Thinking team suggested that, if possible, the same people who participated in the Alignment & Standardization teams should be included in the Implementation phase. This was mandatory for the implementation to be a success. Moreover, clear roles and responsibilities were drafted to insure a smooth transition from theory to practice. Together, local general managers and Implementation Project managers nominated the process group coordinators for all process groups as well as process owners.

Given the reality of a forthcoming implementation, people had a natural tendency to check and re-check their work. Teams from each company began to analyze the processes as they were designed. When the redesigned processes asked for considerably different resources than what had been allocated up until then, teams had to develop down-to-earth plans to bridge that gap. That had to be done by representatives from each company, because up until then, their way of work had been considerably different. If anything could jeopardize the implementation in any way at local level, it could be discussed within the teams.

Implementation teams, process group coordinators and process owners together with all departmental managers established a list of all the employees who were involved in the process. The standardized processes were presented to them and discussed extensively, in order to ensure a clear understanding.

The proposed solutions to the problems that were discovered were discussed locally within the Implementation teams and escalated to the coordinators of national Implementation teams and their team members. So, any requests raised at company level were analyzed and implemented, to preserve the standardized processes at country level.

Any kind of message, including status reports, proposals or requests, followed clear chains of communication: from the local Implementation team to the Implementation manager, and then to the local General Manager; from the local Implementation team to the national process group coordinator, and then to the Project management team. The Continuous Improvement department kept an overview of how the implementation progressed for each process.

Before the Reengineering Project, the objective setting followed only a traditional top-down approach. KPIs cascaded down on the hierarchical Organizational Structure. The transition to the new KPI Architecture will be a fundamental change. The Key Performance Indicators will be horizontally aligned inside processes and vertically aligned throughout process groups.

Each process owner is responsible to work with department managers and with people who performed the roles within processes, to align objectives for Role KPIs. This led to a balance of responsibilities at each level of the company.

For all the aligned and standardized processes, all related documents like: process maps, procedures, work instructions, document templates, and risk analysis have to be developed at country level by the team members. Any specific work instructions and performance indicator targets need to be established by the Local Implementation teams.

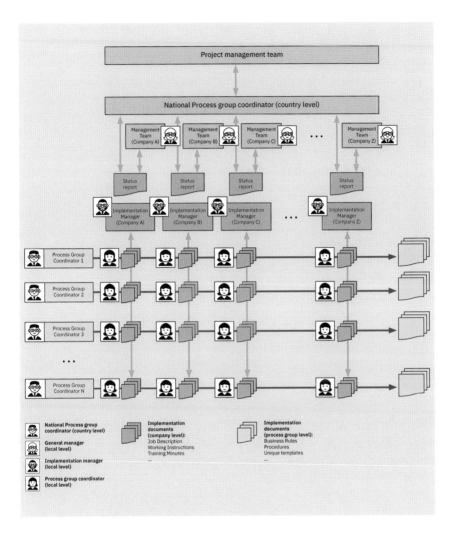

C. Why is This a Better Model?

Let's take a look at everything we've been doing for more than one year and a half and take a deep breath. We climbed a big mountain sprinkled with little rocks made of challenges, difficulties, but also happy moments, celebrations and success. Why do you think this enormous effort worked so well?

First of all, let's take a look at the processes. Before the Synergy phase, there were so many different ways of doing the same work, all considered good in their own way. But was it the best way to do things all around? As an old saying goes, "the more, the merrier"; every process group found the best versions for their processes by taking a joint effort. From now on, people will be working by the same processes, which were customized with the help of knowledge, skills, information and the best practices achieved in the years and years of experience. People will have the same amount and level of information, and they will perform the same activities in different locations. Also, this model of Synergy gives the necessary flexibility for each company to personalize their work instructions according to their actual technology.

Apart from all the arguments for a better model, which were mentioned previously, (standardized processes, KPIs, unitary Risk Management), and which were already implemented, people planted the seeds for a Continuous Improvement culture.

Focusing on People

A mutual and immediate benefit for all those involved in the Project was the fact that they learned to communicate better, to share personal experiences and to rely on each other.

Think about the implications of aligned and standardized roles across all companies. A certain role from a standardized process is assigned to an employee from a department in one company. At the same time, in another company, the same role from the same standardized process can be assigned to an employee from a different department. Why? Because the standardized process remains the same in different companies regardless of the local Organizational Structure, if they really need to be different. Consequently, all skills, knowledge and abilities required for a specific role can now be standardized across all Romanian Veolia companies.

Another positive outcome of the Alignment & Standardization phase was homologizing job listing and core Job Descriptions across all companies. This may increase the workforce mobility by balancing the human resource allocation, based on the different needs of all the companies. This can also ease the "Hire personnel" process.

An aligned and standardized Organizational Architecture creates the means for a unified data-driven evaluation process: everyone would be assessed by the same standards, in an objective and measurable way. Moreover, it sets the premises for an integrated Learning and Development process.

A Proven Organizational Model for Merger and Acquisition

Veolia's presence in Romania is becoming more powerful as new business opportunities arise. For example, a new Romanian company recently joined the

Veolia team as part of its Water Business Line. This company will fully benefit from the new organizational model deployment and all of its know-how. Such an Organizational Architecture, optimized and fully integrated at country level, will represent a tried and tested business model for merger and acquisition.

Joining Hands with Suppliers: Resourcing our Business
Based on the mindset and results achieved in the Alignment & Standardization phase, all the premises of a robust Supply Chain were ready to implement with significant cost and time benefits. This implied finding the common ground for consolidating supply needs from all Veolia companies in Romania and handling them in an integrated way. The next steps will be to find and qualify suppliers in a single portfolio and integrate them into the procurement processes.

And Last but Not Least
All these achievements are set up to be sustainable. Why? Because the result of the Reengineering Project is not something that was imposed, it was the result of the work of hundreds of people who have designed their future together. It has become their child and they will take care of it through the Continuous Improvement strategy. In this way, the processes will no longer be "orphans".

Food for thought:

- How do you create a constructive conversation between multiple organizations with different cultures and perspectives on business?
- How do you create a common language among all those different organizations?
- How do you use this common language to identify, embrace and apply the best practices and to enable synergy?
- What would make a better country setup than the one you already have?

Continuous Improvement in Sight: The Self-Sharpening Organization

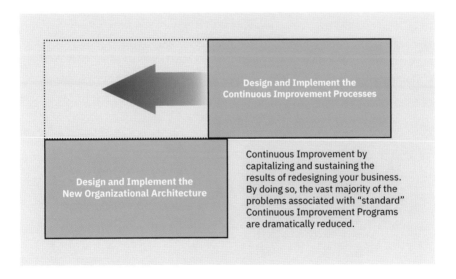

Design and Implement the Continuous Improvement Processes

Design and Implement the New Organizational Architecture

Continuous Improvement by capitalizing and sustaining the results of redesigning your business. By doing so, the vast majority of the problems associated with "standard" Continuous Improvement Programs are dramatically reduced.

1. Decide to Improve: Continuous Improvement – The Strategy to Stay on the Fast Lane

Until this moment, you have been taken on this amazing Journey towards an ambitious goal: to set up an efficient company, able to face the challenges of the

21st century. From the early stages of this Project – as described in Chapter 2 – some of the most involved participants began to have a fear that was difficult to confess: how to maintain the goal, once it's been achieved?

During the days and nights of hard-work, there were some moments of doubt, clustered in questions like: *"And after all this?"*; *"What will happen after this amazing success?"*; *"How should we organize our work in order to keep the state of the art recently set-up in the company?"*; *"Who will drive and manage the necessary changes long after the partners from Advanced Thinking have done their job and take the way of other projects, other challenges?"* The answer was not obvious at all, but it was crystal clear that it was mandatory to have an assurance that the future would not only be bright, but steady.

The solution came naturally and it was certainly not easy and quick to define and to implement. It required time and talent, patience and willingness to learn. It's one of the DNA components of the Master Plan. It needs to be carefully fulfilled in almost all phases of the Project, and through all its deliverables – a clear strategy to maintain and to improve the initial gains had to be set-up as a Continuous Improvement phase.

This is the crown jewel of the whole Project, the assurance of its sustainability. If this is missing, the gains achieved so far will be lost in a flash, as is the case with many other transformation projects in the world.

A. Elements Designed to Continuously Improve

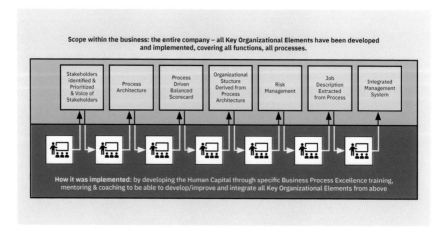

All the organizational elements presented in this book are designed to be excellent for this very moment, for present market conditions, applicable within

existing legal constraints, existing human resources structure, existing technological resources, enablers and so on. But, as we all know and experience,
nothing ever remains unchanged in time.

There are at least two major perspectives to consider so as to continuously
improve: the organizational culture (I), as an enabler for continuously sharpening and improving all organizational elements (II).

I. Organizational Culture is a concept that includes many factors (such as initiative, flexibility, care for customers, responsibility, and discipline) which are
difficult to grasp or control, but which are very well represented among the
enablers of business success. They are also pretty hard to change. Obviously,
the organizational culture influenced the Project in many aspects.

How was it in the very beginning? One member of the top management
team likened their organization with "a semi military type". This might be
assimilated with the "Control-Driven" and "Hierarchical" organizational culture. Is such an organizational culture able to sustain this kind of profound
transformation? The answer is not very encouraging when one really looks at
it: **Risk Management** – "a fragmented and incoherent approach, made only for
specific compliance requirements"; **initiative** – an attitude regarded either as
"impertinent and daring", or as "foolish or crazy" for one "who wants to be promoted at any cost"; **responsibility** – "a job only for managers"; **flexibility** – "only
following our procedures"; **care for customers** – "the customer is a person who
has to comply with our rules, hope and wait for our incredible system to function"; **brand image** – "the reason for the Communication Department to exist".

The need to change all these misguided perceptions became obvious
from the early stages of the Project. Many employees were intimidated, sometimes even felt lost in a long chain of excuses, when trying to formulate decent
answers to questions like: *"How do you contribute to...?"*; *"What do you think about...?"*
They became aware that their company was far behind its potential and market
expectations, so they became even more worried about the company's future
and also their future as professionals.

II. Organizational Elements

The Project offered numerous occasions to learn and raise awareness about
what, why and how we do what we do (or not) within the organization via the
current business activities, but also about what, why and how it would be better to do.

Deliverables and KPIs

Are deliverables produced "first time right"? Are they complete and correct? Deliverables should respond to the specific requests of the stakeholders. Those that don't meet the time and quality criteria are seen as failures. Not meeting the quality criteria adds to the cost of process, known as the cost of poor quality. Its reduction is immediately visible. That's why it needs continuous monitoring and evaluation. Carefully design the requested deliverables, not the unnecessary ones! The reporting system might bring to the surface a huge amount of non-useful, redundant deliverables which are time and energy consuming.

The discovery and use of the graphical and statistical data analysis tools led to results which, at first, ruthlessly reflected the performance of the company at that time – a hard reflection to look at. These were difficult moments, sometimes lived with a mixture of a large range of feelings, starting with shame and ending with black humor: "*is statistics a recognized science or a modern Oracle of Delphi?*" If it's scientific, how can one understand WHEN and WHY things look so bad? How to gain the empowerment to control and to change the current state of affairs? How to transform statistical data and data mining into a useful "advisor" and a powerful predictive tool?

It's easy to understand that statistics and data mining might be valuable allies if the company really wants to know everything about its performance, and if there is a true desire for improvement. To discover, collect and analyze the relevant data requires: intense study, sharp observation, analytical skills and, more importantly, the courage to bring to the surface some unattended issues, responsible for non-performant results.

The minimal prerequisite to ensure the proper conditions for educated data-driven decisions at all management levels is to understand the most appropriate graphical and statistical tools to get the correct diagnostic.

To select and to design a set of representative and sensitive performance indicators requires solid theoretical and also practical knowledge. This is vital to consider in the Process Design phase.

Roles, Responsibilities, Competencies and Job Descriptions

It's the job of the Continuous Improvement phase to lead coherent and integrated improvement initiatives. All improvement actions may lead to consistent changes within the processes; thus, **roles** would be constantly updated and improved, among other elements of the processes. Employees should keep up to date with everything that is required of them, constantly developing

their **competencies** to match the performance targets that must be attained.
Is everyone really aware of all the changes in their roles and **responsibilities**, of all the performance targets that must be attained? Are they properly trained and skilled to execute these roles? Do they have the necessary skills? The answer is in **Job descriptions** and in the **Learning and Development plans**.

Risk Management

Is it a way of spending money for catastrophic events that will never happen? On the contrary, it is a realistic, balanced and prepared response to the identified challenges which a company may face while running their processes. Managing and mitigating risks are another path that leads to improvement projects.

The Integrated Quality Management System

It consists of all the formal internal documents and it is the most appropriate way to express, describe and clarify all of the elements mentioned above and any changes brought to them. This system must be kept alive, in line with every validated change of one or more organizational elements.

B. The Continuous Improvement Process: A Structured Approach

One of the most challenging subjects for an organization is to keep the balance between its resources and its willingness to evolve, to grow. At the same time, the economic, social and legal variations, constraints and opportunities are ever-changing factors that force the company to constantly adjust and adapt its processes.

Change doesn't always have to be abrupt and radical. It can also be an incremental process, based on well-established and transparent rules. It's not that easy to build a business and management culture on this principle. **The temptation of quick and easy implementation of a miraculous technology or organizational solution conceived in 15 minutes of deliberation in a small ad-hoc group is huge and very difficult to prevent.**

Respectable statistic figures indicate that at least 70% of this kind of initiatives are destined to fail at getting the expected results, and could even induce problems which, though unexpected, are difficult to solve. Despite these well-known figures, on each and every organizational level, as a manager or as a simple employee, we all are frequently faced with this type of initiatives. They are not only time-consuming endeavors which require a lot of effort, but are also the main source for unexpected variations in performance, employees' lack of motivation and work satisfaction, and many other negative consequences.

Projects that are managed independently, with different methodologies, based on heterogeneous project execution tools are difficult to monitor and to evaluate on a strategic level. It is generally difficult to get the most appropriate way of achieving good coordination. Yet, one must make it happen. But how? What are the suitable steps to achieve the implementation of such a Continuous Improvement engine?

It is necessary to have a structured approach in order to achieve the best coordination and prioritization of improvement initiatives. It should be managed in a coherent and professional manner, enforced by the full support of top management, and it should execute a well-defined, specific group of processes.

The major components of the Continuous Improvement process group are: the Project Selection process, the Project Execution process and the Project Portfolio Management process. To properly execute improvement projects, people need to be constantly able to develop through the Learning and Development process. The Project Selection process must take into consideration the negative signals on the company's dashboard, mainly its traced process nonconformities and process variation.

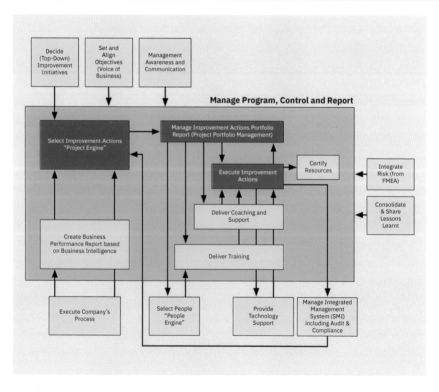

Having well represented internal high competencies like 8D, Lean Six Sigma, Business Process Management, etc. isn't only a reason for pride, but a confirmation of the strength of the organization, its resilience and ability to evolve.

Continuous Improvement represents, in fact, a process group with the main goal of fulfilling the best conditions to ensure an organic evolution of the designed and implemented Organizational Architecture, element by element, according to the strategic objectives of the company and its business environment. The quality and accuracy of the process design and execution are the key enablers for success.

Also, the will to design and execute the Continuous Improvement processes becomes undoubtedly a key factor to motivate the teams of employees to work in the Project, bearing in mind that the results of their efforts will last, will be maintained and developed as necessary.

And the whole Project team will have a treasurer of the internal center of excellence and knowledge base as a constant interlocutor, to facilitate and sustain all the changes or improvement initiatives.

2. Act to Improve: The Execution of the Continuous Improvement Process Group

Continuous Improvement was integrated from the early phases of the Reengineering Project as a valuable solution, acting as a "laboratory" for maintaining and developing the company's most important resources, the main tool to ensure its ascending trend.

The most sensitive subject – which triggered long debates – was responsibility, which was thoroughly addressed and finally clarified. In some cases, it was the subject of many meetings, sometimes creating a tense atmosphere and long and uneasy debates. The most helpful questions in this respect (facilitating and at the same time provoking) were: *"What is the voice of the process?"* and *"Who triggers the process?"*

As previously mentioned in this book, to use the most appropriate graphical and statistical data analysis tools, a dedicated software application was deployed in the company and people were trained to use it. Data from the processes within the company was also used during the training, which offered a true understanding of the performance level. This was an important incentive for process owners to become well-informed and able to cure processes, to propose and to take decisions based on real data, rather than on feelings or undocumented external advice.

Therefore, this also strongly strengthened the moral authority to present and to sustain all the necessary decisions. For employees, painful decisions were even more easily accepted due to the reliability of data-driven decisions.

A pleasant surprise, which confirmed success, came with the first invitation to participate to a Lean Six Sigma Yellow Belt training course. The final number of attendees was three times more than planned. These numbers speak for themselves: people were interested and willing to learn. They were going to become advocates to defend their results. The Project management team could be proud.

In order to have an integrated system to lead the improvement projects, an organization must have a dedicated team and methodology. The coordination of this team should be allocated from the highest level in the organization and sustained by the entire management team. It was named the Continuous Improvement department and was set-up during the early stages of the second phase of the Project.

The Continuous Improvement department took the role of the first internal operational leader of the improvement projects, the knowledge base receptor and treasurer, the internal high-level coordinator of the main project activities, and the process owner of the Continuous Improvement process group.

One of its first objectives was to initiate the selection and validation of the proposals for the Operational Board, a cross-company working group of experts. It was designated to evaluate and to coordinate all the improvement initiatives, starting with the problem statement until the final validation for the execution of a project. The Operational Board members were selected based on several simple criteria: their contribution to the Project, their results in the Lean Six Sigma Yellow Belt examination and their professional profile, in order to have a multidisciplinary team of people who can understand and judge all the problem statements that were submitted and their respective improvement projects.

The Operational Board had to prepare all the project proposals for management approval, suggesting the most appropriate priorities for budget allocation. One of the key members of the Operational Board, the financial controller, was in charge of proposing financial models and KPIs for all projects and to verify all the financial figures during project execution and, in the end, to forecast the return on investment ratio.

The Operational Board members were the first team trained for the Lean Six Sigma Green Belt. The practical and innovative approach was to include the design of the most important Continuous Improvement processes in the context of the Green Belt training. The process identification and design were done in the same spirit, based on the methodology we have described so far.

At the same time, the Continuous Improvement team worked to put in place practical IT tools to manage its processes in a transparent way. A series of surveys were launched to gather the necessary information.

The Operational Board and the Continuous Improvement team must deal with and lead the ENTIRE improvement projects portfolio of the company, meaning a considerable budget and key expectations for the company, no matter the technological layer involved. The effort is substantial, but the benefits balance it out. It is all a matter of sustaining high competencies and sharp rigor.

Soon, according to the approved Project strategy, all these things must be extended to all Romanian Veolia Companies. This will happen after the first wave of improvement projects at Apa Nova will be successfully executed. Based on the new Organizational Architecture, the Continuous Improvement Journey has only now truly begun. Will it be an exciting trip full of surprises or the precise development of a well-designed plan? Or will it be both?

Food for thought:

- How would you embed the Continuous Improvement mindset in the DNA of your organization?
- What are the critical levers to support improvement initiatives?

Take Away Thoughts: A View from the Outside-In

Consider this: transforming any organization into a world leader is no small task. Doing this against a historic backdrop involving the legacy of political heritage (Communism, state control, utilities mindset), culture, customer expectations and regulatory environment – yes, a challenge most would baulk at. However, this story has heroes and heroines at every level, ranging from those who had the vision and established the original successful outcomes, to the people on the ground, who have worked diligently, tirelessly to implement the new ways, and the exemplary leadership team who has had the courage to look beyond the staid traditional performance indicators to embrace a new way.

Initially on the path less trodden, they have created a formula that others can emulate, a repeatable, robust and systematic means to transform any organization into a capable, flexible, agile and proactive entity able to meet not only the immediate challenges, but to also go the extra mile and prepare for an uncertain future that few can predict.

This is the collaborative work of many hearts and souls who had the courage and self-belief to know they were creating something very special, something beyond a case study, something that is truly transformational.

The seismic shift, at its fundamental level, was moving from an industrial age, functional view of business, to a "process view" able to liberate people from the confines of their functional silos and encourage them to collaborate to achieve successful outcomes. And yes, if you did that locally, good on you! However, with all the politics of a large, previously cumbersome enterprise with a traditional awards system that praised task orientation, this was far more difficult.

Overcoming the constraints wasn't then just a management edict, it was and is the collective effort of hundreds of people and teams in many diverse environments, shifting their thinking and actions into the customer age.

The challenge of telling this story is distilling it to its essence. What makes this any different and how could it help you to replicate, nay, understand the method and you yourself go the extra mile to take these learnings and transform yourself and your business?

Having had the privilege to witness the transformation, and in the spirit of sharing the learning, we would suggest the following:

1. Get everyone, and yes, we do mean everyone, onside

Disney refer to something called "True North Alignment". It doesn't matter whether you are the janitor or a C-Level executive, everyone knows where you are pointing as an enterprise and, from a day-to-day operational standpoint, you can assess everything anyone is doing to ensure they keep the needle pointing towards True North.

Yes, there will be days when the sky falls in, but are all of you pushing in the right direction?

2. Metrics. What gets measured gets done

This is painful because **most of what we traditionally measure reinforces that industrial age mindset.** You have to step back from those measures and reassess, with a process management view and mindset: is this stuff helping us get to where we need to be?

3. There will be casualties

"Nothing in the world is worth having or worth doing unless it means effort, pain and difficulty." Theodore Roosevelt

Most likely, we all follow the classic cycle when we try to do something worthy and big. It is simply human nature that, when faced with seemingly insurmountable obstacles and pressure, we throw in the towel.

However, emerging from those many are a few courageous people who have seen the light, understand the process vision, and despite their circumstances, fight to deliver their part. That's what this has all been about when enough people rejected the old functional ways and embraced the new leadership vision to liberate the processes and to reengineer, to achieve something special, something world-beating.

4. Connect the dots and draw the lines

At an operational level, linking strategy to day-to-day operations through business lines, process owners, process groups and activities is a clearly desirable objective. Also, understanding the relevance of the business rules that underpin all activity is key in ensuring not just the ability to perform the reengineered processes, but actual compliance to regulations. Drawing the lines of these linkages ensures significant improvements to productivity and enhanced control, noting again that these two objectives work hand in hand.

Creating this robust architecture is critical to firstly implementing the new way and subsequently maintaining and developing it further.

5. It is all about the people (after all)

It would be easy to focus all attention on getting the processes "right", but the main enabling element is the employees truly "getting it" and understanding their roles within a new paradigm. No longer are they perceived as just task masters; they are now liberated to participate in all improvement efforts, from the board room to the lunchroom, and given the remit to propose and implement ongoing improvements.

For the future, this shift in responsibilities, away from task management to outcome delivery, creates the elusive environment of Continuous Improvement. No longer are instructions awaited from on high; instead, employees identify the needed change and further improvements are incorporated and integrated rapidly by the people on the ground, in coordination with other groups and processes.

Ultimately, the creation of this self-managing ecosystem is the guarantee that the enterprise will continue to evolve and mature in tandem with the changes in society. It is this real shift from being reactive to anticipating and embracing the future that ensures Veolia's long-term success.

Leadership

During the Project, Veolia leadership and management team set a clear and concise vision which cascaded, along with the process strategy and plan, over every nook and cranny of the enterprise. In many instances, that vision to action delivered ahead of plan, with a momentum enthusiastically embraced by all. The venture to transform and the ongoing success was reinforced on the global stage with Veolia being acknowledged not just as an industry leader, but also across all sectors[3].

That endorsement for the Project has helped to ensure the continuing commitment of the employees to complete all activities with the certainty of leadership approval. We all know too well the story of organizations that didn't make the transition to the modern way, getting themselves stuck by just trying to improve what they already knew.

Global giants – now gone, or a shadow of their former selves, including Kodak, Nokia, Motorola, Blackberry et al. – have now become a footnote in business history case studies. Contrast that with what Apa Nova achieved in accepting the challenge and transformation to Outside-In thinking and delivery. It has reset the global bar across all sectors.

---

3   The OPEX conference held annually in Orlando, Florida, where Veolia won the prestigious award, "Best Business Transformation Project", acknowledging the rigour, depth and breadth of their transformation.

Philippe Guitard is a graduate engineer from Polytech' Montpellier and holds a qualified graduation in hydrobiology. He started his career in industrial water treatment in 1985, joining the Veolia Group. From 1988 to 1995, he was in charge of water operations in Dordogne and Cannes and the Nice regions. Nominated at Puerto Rico, from 1995 to 1997, he was regional director in Ponce de Leon. In 1997, he moved to the Czech Republic and was appointed CEO of Veolia Water for the Czech Republic in 1999 and CEO of Veolia Water for Central Europe and Russia in 2002. In 2008, he was appointed Director of Veolia Water Europe (excluding France). In 2013, he was appointed Senior Executive Vice President in Central and Eastern Europe for water waste and energy and is a member of the Executive Committee. Passionate about fishing and mycology, Philippe Guitard lives Veolia's singular vision of the world both in his public and private life.

Jorj-Mădălin Mihailovici is the CEO of Veolia Romania. Mădălin has vast Leadership and Management experience, holding key Top Executive positions over the last 15 years. His results over the years make him one of the most wanted CEOs on the market. His passion for empowering people led to a 28-year University career, a Ph.D. in Technical Sciences – Hydrotechnical Constructions and dozens of books, articles and conferences. He has represented Romania in organizations such as the European Federation of National Associations of Water Services and the United Nations Environment Program – Dams and development project. As a worldwide international recognition, he received the Gold Medal at the Geneva International Invention Exhibition in 2016, and the title of Commander (Number of the cross: 19 101) at the European Innovation Awards in 2017.

Irina Munteanu is the Chief Financial Officer for Veolia Romania. After starting her professional career with TMF and KPMG, Irina moved to Veolia's Apa Nova where – based on her native Leadership skills – she rapidly went from Financial Controller to becoming the Veolia CFO in Romania in 2013. She has vast experience with financial reporting, including IFRS, Statutory and US GAAP financial statements, taxes and treasury management. Based on her sharp business skills and innovative perspectives – invaluable to any team she has been part of or led – she was appointed, in 2019, as the Co-Lead of the "One Veolia Project Romania", the biggest ever Business Transformation effort involving all Veolia entities in Romania.

Cristian Matei is the Co-Founder and President of Advanced Thinking, and he serves as Senior Leadership Advisor, Coach and Consultant, having extensive experience in working on all continents with Executive Boards requiring expert assistance in improving organizational performance. He is a former Global Head Learning and Development at General Electric and former Global Head Operational Quality & Continuous Improvement at Alstom. He owns a Ph.D. in Organizational Architecture Reengineering & Business Transformation, a double Lean Six Sigma Master Black Belt certification with Six Sigma Academy and Alstom and was named the Operational Excellence European Contributor of the year 2011.

Steve Towers was named one of the 15 most influential Global Customer Service Experts in 2019. He is an experienced business transformation leader with over 40 years of success in driving and achieving organizational goals in both the private and public sectors, in a variety of key "C" leadership and top-level consulting positions. He was awarded the Process Excellence Community Contributor of the year (2018) and Lifetime Achievement Award (2007), and is recognized across industries, including Business Process Management, Enterprise Architecture, Customer Experience and Lean Six Sigma.

References

ARTICLES

Burke, W. W., Litwin, G. H., 1992, "A causal model of organizational performance and change", *Journal of Management*

Csaszar, Felipe A., 2012, "Organizational structure as a determinant of performance", *Strategic Management Journal*

Hannan, M. T., Freeman J., 1984, "Structural inertia and organizational change", *American Sociological Review*

Martinez-Leon, I. M., 2011, "The influence of organizational structure on organizational learning", *International Journal of Manpower*, Vol. 32, No. 5/6

Ogbona E., Harris L. C., 2003, "Innovative organizational structures and performance", *Journal of Organizational Change Management*, Vol. 16, No. 5

Ouchi, W. G., 1977, "The relationship between organizational structure and organizational control", *Administrative Science Quarterly*

BOOKS

Aguayo, R., 1990, *Dr. Deming: the American who taught the Japanese about quality*, First Carol Publishing Edition

Barrett, R., 1998, *Liberating the corporate soul*, Butterwoth-Heinemann

Daft, R. L., 1998, *Organization theory and design,* 6th edn, South-Western College Publishing

Deming, W. E., 1994, *The new economics for industry, government, education*, 2nd edn, The MIT Press

Drucker, P. F., 1999, *Management challenges for the 21st century*, Butterworth – Heinemann

Etzioni, A., 1961, *A comparative analysis of complex organizations*, Free Press

Freeman, E. R., 2010, *Strategic management*, Cambridge University Press

George, M., 2003, *Lean Six Sigma for service, chapter 1-the ROI of Lean Six Sigma for services*, McGraw-Hill Professional

Hammer, M., 1996, *Beyond reengineering*, Harper Collins

Hammer, M., 2001, *The agenda*, 1st edn, Crown Business

Hammer, M., and Champy, J., 1993, *Reengineering the corporation*, HarperCollins

172   Handy, C., 2001, *Elefantul și puricele*, Codecs

Imai, M., 2007, *Gemba Kaizen: a commonsense, low-cost approach
to management*, McGraw-Hill Professional

Juran, J. M., and Defeo, J., 2014, *Juran's quality essentials
for leaders*, McGraw-Hill Education

Kaplan, R. S., and Norton D .P., 1996, *The balanced
scorecard*, Harvard College Press

Laszlo, E., 1996, *The systems view of the world*, Hampton Press

Liker, J. K., and Franz J. K., 2011, *The Toyota way to continuous
improvement: linking strategy and operational excellence to
achieve superior performance*, McGraw-Hill Professional

Liker, J. K., and Meier, D., 2005, *The Toyota way
fieldbook*, McGraw-Hill Education

McChrystal, G. S. et al., 2015, *Team of teams: new rules
of engagement for a complex world*, Penguin

Naim, M., 2013, *The End of Power*, Basic Books

Peters, T. J., and Waterman, R. H., 1984, *In search of excellence: lessons
from America's best-run companies*, Harper Business Essentials

Porter, M., 2008, *Competitive strategy: techniques for analyzing
industries and competitors*, Simon and Schuster

Pugh, D. S., and Hickson, D. J., 1989, *Writers on
organizations,* Harmondsworth: Penguin

Radu, I., Lefter, V., Șendroiu, C., Ursăcescu, M., and Cioc, M., 2009,
*Effects of the public-private partnership in water supply and
sewerage public services. Experience of the municipality of Bucharest,*
Publishing House of the Academy of Economic Studies

Radu, I., Șendroiu, C., 2013, *The effects of the public private
partnership in the public water supply and sewerage services
of Bucharest (2008–2012)*, Editura Universitară

Savage, C. M., 1996, *5th Generation management*, Butterworth-Heinemann

Senge, P., 1999, *The dance of change*, DoubleDay

Senge, P., 2006, *The fifth discipline*, DoubleDay

Slywotzky, A. J., and Weber, K., 2011, *Demand: creating what people
love before they know they want it*, Crown Business

Towers, S., and Fingar, P., 2003, *In search of BPM excellence:
straight from the thought leaders*, Meghan Kiffer Press

Towers, S., 1995, *Business process re-engineering – a senior
executives guide*, Nelson Thornes Ltd.

Towers, S., 2010, *Outside-in. The secret of the 21st century leading companies*, 3rd edn, BP Group Publishing

Towers, S., and Dodkins, J., 2015, *The process tactics playbook*, available at lulu.com

Womack, J. P., et al., 2011, *The machine that changed the world*, Simon and Schuster

Printed in Great Britain
by Amazon